PAWS FOR THOUGHT:

A Look at the Conflicts, Questions and Challenges of Animal Euthanasia

— B.J. Ellis —

Paw Print Press

©1993
Paw Print Press
All rights reserved
Printed in the United States of America

No part of this book, except for brief excerpts for review purposes, may be reproduced, in any form or by any means, electronic, mechanical, photocopied or otherwise, without the written permission of the publisher.

Paw Print Press
7509-I Garners Ferry Road
Suite 164
Columbia SC 29209

Typesetting and page layout
by
John D. Marshall

10 9 8 7 6 5 4 3 2 1
ISBN: 0-9636708-0-8

Dedication:

To all the people who must make difficult decisions about animals.

Table of Contents

Acknowledgments 7
Preface 9

Section 1: Introduction   18
   Reality Check 18
   Society's Dirty Work 20

Section 2: Euthanasia   26
   Be the Best We Can Be — But It Ain't Easy 26
   Push the Green Button and Walk Away 28
   Misuse of Injection Method 30
   Dealing With Co-Workers 32
   How to Deal with the Guilt 33
   The D Zone 35
   Frequently Asked Questions 41
   For People in Wildlife Rehabilitation and Rescue
      Who Are Faced With Euthanasia 52
   Laboratory Technicians and Research Animals 57
   The Euthanasia Room 60
   Suggestions for Co-Workers Who Don't have to
      Euthanize Animals 61
   If You Volunteer at a Shelter 62
   Summary 63

Section 3: Voices: Us and Them   66
   Us 66
      From the Trenches 71
      Truth in Advertising 74
      People are Watching Us 74
   Them 75

Section 4: Feelings, Emotions 78
  Times are changing 81
  Let's Talk About Grief 82
  Stages of Grief 83
  How to Start a Support Group 85
  Finding a Facilitator 87
  Employee Assistance Program Advice 88
  Stress Busters 90
  Exercises for Individuals or Groups 90

Section 5: Paws for Thought 94
  Poems, Prayers and Editorials 94

Section 6: The Challenges Ahead 110
  Survival: Burn Out or Rust Out? 110
  Dealing With the Public 111
  Role of Animal Shelters in the Future 117
  Honor the Animals—and Yourself 117
  Ten Rational Plans of Action for the Pet
    Overpopulation Crisis 119

Section 7: Resource Guide 122
  Consultants on Euthanasia Stress 122
  Reference Material 125
  Bibliography 125
  Glossary 133

About the Author 137

Acknowledgments

Special thanks go to many people and their respective organizations for assisting along the way. That includes:

- Patti Judd, Euthanasia Technician and author of "Shelter Worker's Credo."
- Abigail Van Buren, "Dear Abby," for granting permission to reprint two of her columns and for being a friend.
- Dennis Fetko, Ph.D., "Dr. Dog" with prayers and wishes for your recovery.
- Phil Arkow, of the Humane Society of the Pikes Peak Region, Colorado Springs, for sharing his coping mechanisms.
- Karen Stickland for her contributions to the section on support groups and for encouraging me to not give up this project.
- Doug Fakkema for his longtime commitment to proper ET training and easing euthanasia stress.
- Carter Luke for his survival tips and dedication to the "Year of the Cat."
- Randall Lockwood and Marc Paulhus at The Humane Society of the United States for their continued work in this area.
- Bill Hurt Smith for his dedication to the ETs and officers in the field, and special thanks for granting permission to use Barbara Hurst Smith's poems.
- Jane Ehrhardt, American Humane Association for providing research material and resource people.

In South Carolina, thanks to Eloise McMillan and Henry Brzezinski for their leadership qualities and commitment to the humane treatment of animals. Personally, thanks and hugs to Dr. Frank Provenzano for his belief in me and sharing stress management advice. To my brothers, Tom and Matt, and my sister, Mary, who always bring joy to my life and make me proud to be their sister. On the homefront, all my love to my husband, John, for his support, devotion and encouragement. To my companion cats Kitteena Marina and Tigerooey-Baby, for their constant source of companionship and moments of pleasant distraction from my long hours at the computer.

Preface

"Why this book?"
Consider these recent statistics:

- The average length a person has a dog is five years.
- The average length a person has a cat is four years.
- The average age of a dog turned into an animal shelter is one year or younger.

We live in a throw away society. Americans tend to have a "hate/love" relationship with their pets.

One moment Fluffy is a cherished family member. The next moment, he or she is just an inconvenience to be dumped—usually with her most recent litter of puppies or kittens.

"I know you'll find good homes for them," the soon-to-be-former pet owner says. However, if Fluffy has to be put to sleep, "Don't tell me about it!"

Millions of loving pets must be destroyed each year because people neither want them nor love them enough to take proper care of them.

Pet owners can be extremely apathetic, irresponsible and downright abusive. They can neglect to spay or neuter their pets. Or they want their children to experience the "miracle of birth." Some abandon the poor animals or let their dogs wander off. Others believe that feeding a stray cat at their back door is the limit of their responsibility to the feline. Yet other factors contribute to the dog and cat overpopulation crisis:

- Backyard breeders who want to recoup their investment.
- Intentional overbreeding in puppy mills, by hobby breeders and professional breeders. And defiant national dog and cat breeder organizations that are unwilling to admit they contribute to the problem.
- Pet shop owners who buy animals from puppy mills and cat factories.
- Pet food companies. A billion dollar industry that subtly encourages pet overbreeding in its advertising in order to increase sales of their product.
- Veterinarians who oppose low cost spay/neuter clinics.
- Animal shelters for training the public too well to bring in their unwanted animals and for not saying the "E" word around the public.
- Shelters that allow unaltered animals to be adopted.

This list could go on and on.

It's easy to point the finger of blame. At times I blame myself for not adopting more animals, not volunteering at the local shelter more or not donating more money to humane causes.

Because of these factors, animal shelters must deal with unwanted animals on a daily basis.

Throughout the country, agencies grapple with the health and safety hazards of unwanted and uncontrolled animals.

Preface

Thousands of community animal shelters are bulging with forgotten and abandoned dogs and cats, the disposable victims of a "throw-away" society. Rabies outbreaks, interrupted mail service, livestock and game losses—these are the results of animal control problems.

There's a lot going on in animal welfare and animal protection these days. Most of the work is done quietly behind the scenes.

Carrying out animal control policies is tough. People can be extremely emotional and unreasonable when it comes to animals.

When a shelter does attract the media's attention it's when the wrong dog is euthanized. Why doesn't the media get enraged about the millions of unwanted animals that are destroyed annually?

Or an Animal Control Officer will get in the news chasing after a tiger or elephant escaped from the zoo or circus. Or the officer has to remove a pet snake from under somebody's house.

Groups like the National Animal Control Association, The Humane Society of the U.S., the American Humane Association and others constantly work to upgrade the profession by providing training, certification and information .

The harsh reality for most shelter workers is that there is too much work, not enough money and never enough understanding from "civilians" or outsiders.

They must deal with a generally apathetic public or with animal rights extremists who offer no logical solutions, only to "liberate" the animals. Or the segment of people who believe animals don't deserve any rights at all.

The "no-kill" animal shelter operators who provide a warehouse-style caged existence for animals. And don't forget the animal collectors, who take in any and all strays with little regard to animal health.

There are so many diverse groups, each with their own agenda. One group spawns another group. Each issue creates a backlash.

There is very little middle ground. And animal welfare workers are confronted with it all.

Until there is a drastic improvement in the pet overpopulation problem, a significant part of an Animal Control Officer's job will involve destroying healthy animals. The effect is to put ordinary people under extraordinary stress.

Euthanasia is the leading cause of death for dogs and cats in the U.S. And Euthanasia Stress is one of the biggest causes of burnout among Animal Control Officers and Euthanasia Technicians.

But euthanasia is not limited to cats and dogs. Skunks, raccoons, possums, snakes, horses, mice, birds and other creatures at times have to be destroyed because they are considered "nuisances" and can't be released into the wild because of serious injuries or other reasons.

Again, the fate of that animal's life is in your hands.

You came to work here because you love animals, why do you have to kill them? The first rule is, there are no rules. That is one of the many conflicts of working with animals.

For example, don't get attached to the animal, don't look IT in the eye. Don't give IT a name. Easy to intellectualize but not in reality.

That's why I wrote this book. It's a forum to examine those conflicts, get in touch with those feelings and find ways to deal with them.

This book is for the hard-working animal abuse investi-

Preface

gators. The ones who keep a bottle in their desk to ease their psychic pain. The ones I've overheard bragging about their drunken all-nighters. The ones who are in the doghouse with their spouses because they've given up trying to explain why they feel so bad.

This book will primarily address the conflicts experienced by animal shelter workers. Many shelters have wildlife centers for rescue and rehabilitation. That's why I am also including research laboratory technicians and wildlife rehabilitators in this book. These people are often faced with having to euthanize animals they have tended to for many years. Or they must euthanize an injured raptor because the creature cannot survive in the wild.

So many people are faced with difficult decisions about animals.

I am compelled to write this book. In whatever ways, I hope this book can help you, a person committed to animal protection, welfare and rehabilitation to examine your conflicts about euthanasia. That it will help you acknowledge your grief, loss and anger.

I hope this book will provide you with resources and networking information. You are not alone.

That in reading it, you will be able to make some sense out of the pet overpopulation crisis and know you are making a difference.

And that you will not give up.

I expect some people to attack this book. They won't like it because this isn't a politically correct subject and no-kill supporters won't like it for obvious reasons. But I didn't write it to please anybody.

I wrote it hoping to help people, specifically the ones who must make difficult decisions about animals. I have

Paws for Thought

talked with dozens of hard-working caring individuals who are committed to helping animals. They love animals, but they have to kill them. How unfair. How stressful.

In writing this book, I tried to compile a variety of resources, experts and opinions on the subject of euthanasia. I looked for books that could be helpful resources.

I am not a Euthanasia Technician. But I have participated in injection euthanasia on puppies and dogs. I have observed euthanasia of dogs in a carbon monoxide chamber.

I have attended euthanasia workshops conducted by Bill Smith, Doug Fakkema and by the South Carolina Animal Care and Control Association.

I have walked in "The D Zone," as Smith calls it.

Dozens of ETs and shelter workers have poured their hearts out to me about their stresses, hurts and conflicts of this situation.

I am not a veterinarian or medically trained technician. But I know that today's ETs are expected to be able to use needles, mix solutions together and know where and how to inject all that in an animal.

They are also expected to learn it quickly and carry out their duties humanely. Again and Again.

My intent was to talk to all kinds of people who deal with humane euthanasia to provide a variety of "voices" on the subject. That includes: veterinarians, animal control officers, animal behaviorists, sociologists, wildlife rehabilitators, laboratory technicians, shelter directors, kennel staffers, volunteers and plenty of Euthanasia Technicians, of course.

I wanted a variety of answers and opinions. Because it's important to realize there are many options and not just

Preface

one way to approach these conflicts and challenges. In the end, the only person who knows how they feel about animal euthanasia is *YOU*.

—*B.J. Ellis*
April 1993

Goals of this book:

- Increase awareness of Euthanasia Stress.

- Provide answers to frequently asked questions about euthanasia.

- Affirm what Euthanasia Technicians are doing. Discuss ways to deal with Euthanasia Stress and provide tools to help.

- Talk about feelings and emotions, especially dealing with unresolved grief.

- Take control of your situation. It's time to take pride in your job and not accept the blame or society's guilt.

- Take time to "Paws for Thought." Listen to others. Speak out Yourself. You are Not Alone.

- Think about the challenges ahead. How to survive in this field. Do something about the problem.

- Become part of a network. Be the best you can be. Know who to call, where to attend workshops, what books to read.

Section 1:
Introduction

Introduction

Reality Check
Who lives? Who dies?
The Ultimate Conflict

"I can't bear to kill another animal."

More than eight million animals a year die in the arms of the people who had hoped to save them. That is a bitter reality that every caring person inside and outside a shelter hates.

Every day at shelters across the country, animals must be evaluated: who stays, who goes?

These life-or-death decisions wear shelter managers down. The act of killing animals contributes to burnout and job turnover. Animal rights groups and most of the public blame the shelters for killing healthy animals.

> "Euthanasia technicians are charged with the responsibility of providing a 'painless' and 'merciful' death. However, what may be a physically painless death for the animals may be a psychologically painful event for the euthanasia technicians...To understand the psychological pain experienced by a person who must euthanize animals one must first understand the contradiction inherent in the job...Euthanizing animals is one of the most challenging and yet undesirable services performed by animal control personnel. On the one hand, they

Introduction

> must hold a special interest in the well-being of animals; on the other hand, they must purposely destroy animals. The task of killing an animal is further complicated by the fact that some animals disposed of are not necessarily dangerous, diseased or antisocial."
>
> From: *The Psychology of Euthanizing Animals: The Emotional Components* by Charles E. Owens, Ricky Davis and Bill Hurt Smith, 1981.

"I can't bear to see another dead animal on the highway."

"I know if I pick up that stray dog, he'll just be euthanized."

"I'm tired of excuses from the people who bring in animals. I hate people."

Does that sound like something you might say?

Away from the shelter and during off-hours, do you avoid contact with "civilians" because they call you a "puppy killer."

Do you engage in self-destructive behavior such as drinking too much or having suicidal thoughts?

Do you want to sleep all the time or sleep too little?

When you do fall asleep, do you wake up having a nightmare?

There's no one to talk to. Your family, friends and even some of your co-workers don't understand what you're going through.

You don't understand yourself.

"Go kill that dog and be nice to those people."

Does that sound like your boss?
You wonder why you ever took this job.
"Why did you pick that puppy? He was my favorite," whines a co-worker as you leave the euthanasia room.
"Don't question me. It's my job," you reply.
Many "civilian" people have asked me why I am writing this book. Anyone who has spent time working or volunteering at an animal shelter is hungry for information on this topic. They want to talk about *IT*.
Death is the topic. *IT* is euthanasia. Those are not topics for polite conversation.
Look at the terms we use for euthanasia: "put down," "put to sleep," "dispatched."
But enormous changes have taken place in animal shelters in just the past decade. Ready or not, the public is no longer going to be spared what goes on in shelters anymore.
This book is for the individuals who work with animals to help them sort out their feelings and hopefully feel better about themselves.

Society's Dirty Work

First of all, you are to be commended for working in this field. Your job is one of the most misunderstood and least appreciated by the public.
Like policemen, you usually see people at their worst. You don't get thanked for doing your job. You only get criticized and then that's done publicly in the media or at a county council meeting.
The ultimate irony here is that you are attracted to the field because you love animals, but have to kill them. You

Introduction

are caught between the animal rights extremists and the animal abusers.

This book is for you: to help you, give you hope, prevent burnout and help you take care of yourself.

You are there to provide a humane, dignified death for an animal nobody wanted and that was bred unnecessarily.

You get criticized for being a puppy killer, dog catcher and cat killer.

A bona fide humane society accepts all animals regardless of health, age and temperament. Private shelters can be selective and accept only those animals they believe can be sold or placed into a new home.

The awful truth is, there are simply not enough good homes to keep up with the excess animals.

The Humane Society of the United States estimates 70,000 kittens and puppies are born every day compared to 10,000 human births. The harsh reality of these statistics is that even if everyone who wanted animals was responsible enough to keep one, there would still be thousands of animals without a home.

Anyone who has spent any time working or volunteering at an animal shelter eventually has to face the fact that millions of dogs and cats must be euthanized each year because there are no homes for them.

Some people have great difficulty accepting the fact that unwanted animals are euthanized. Those people may be your family, friends or even co-workers.

They see the kindness in euthanizing an animal that is in great pain, or terminally ill. But why must young, healthy puppies and kittens be put to sleep?

Why can't they be kept at a "no-kill" shelter indefinitely? Isn't that better than euthanasia?

In many cases, no. Cats and dogs thrive on companionship. While they may receive adequate shelter, food and water, they need affection and human attention.

As Animal Control Officers and Euthanasia Technicians, your objective is to prevent and free animals from suffering. Death, humanely administered is not bad, but a kindness to animals that are unwanted and suffering in isolation.

Companionship is one of the basic needs of dogs, cats, horses or any domesticated animal.

It is difficult to euthanize animals, especially for those of us who love animals. I have participated in euthanasia by injection and it hurts to see the life pushed out of a sentient creature. But it hurts more to see a starving puppy or kitten digging in a garbage can or to drive by a dead animal on the highway.

That's why I support humane euthanasia when it is done by a properly trained technician. I do not like it and neither do the ETs.

ACOs and ETs must contend daily with their personal reactions to euthanasia. Some 8,000 to 10,000 individuals work in these positions at the estimated 4,000 animal shelters across the country.

Euthanasia Stress is one of the biggest causes of burnout among staff, but it's often the least talked about or understood. It's controversial. The public blames shelters. Animal rights groups protest euthanasia.

Humane societies and shelters are taking stronger stands with hard-hitting ad campaigns and calling for voluntary breeding bans.

"We're tired of putting these healthy animals down," says Janet Collier, manager of Tri-Lakes Animal Humane Society in Saranac Lake, New York. "It's time to put the

Introduction

responsibility on the public and the pet owner."
It is a reality that many shelter personnel across the country are determined to change.

"It's time to be honest with the public," says Merry Ellen Poole, director of Animal Control and Humane Treatment at Montgomery County, Maryland, Animal Control. "For years we didn't talk about euthanasia. We didn't want to tell sad stories. We told them, 'we'll find them a good home.' We were afraid we wouldn't get donations."

Now we call it killing healthy animals. It's not just the shelter's problem. It's everybody's problem.

Fortunately, thanks to effective spay/neuter campaigns, the number of animals euthanized is decreasing. But what about the humans whose job is to kill animals?

As animal lovers, we have the responsibility to release unwanted animals from suffering. Death should be as painless and comfortable as possible.

I don't expect to see the problems caused by pet overpopulation solved any time soon.

That's why I believe this book is important. It's time to talk about a subject that no one has wanted to talk about. It's time to acknowledge what you are doing and quit taking the blame for what irresponsible pet ownership has created.

Over the years, technology has improved, allowing for a more "humane death" for the animal rather than slow, painful "gas chamber" death.

But the price that had to be paid for this advancement is that the human technician is required to participate far more intimately than his/her predecessors ever did. Each animal has to be held and restrained in order to accomplish the injection to bring about the quick loss of consciousness from sodium pentobarbital. Dogs quite often lick the Euthanasia Technicians hands or face before collapsing. What can shelters do to protect their staff? When a new staff member is brought on board, the administration should ensure that he or she be thoroughly trained. Stress within the workplace can be drastically reduced if staff training is intense and complete. Training should include discussions of ethical, not just technical, subjects. The staff should understand their individual roles within the shelter. They should understand the role of the shelter within the community.

Their frustrations and anxieties over these matters are normal. And how they deal with these frustrations are vital. Regular staff meetings to vent feelings are important. Ideally, employee assistance programs and support groups should be available to ETs.

Now is the time to put yourself first, you are important!

Section 2:
Euthanasia

Euthanasia

Be the Best We Can Be — But It Ain't Easy

> "In our training, we teach this concept: the animal did not ask to be born; it did not ask to go to the shelter, and it certainly did not ask to die. Within the framework of our own human limitations and resources, we owe the animal the best possible death."
>
> From: *The Handbook of Pentobarbital Euthanasia*, Tim Greyhavens, Humane Society of the Willamette Valley.

In 1971, within five minutes of his first humane society job in Eugene, Oregon, Doug Fakkema put his first animal to death. Nine months later he took over as executive director of Benton Humane Society in Corvallis, Oregon.

For several months, Fakkema destroyed animals, with minimal training and without any knowledge of what they were feeling or what was happening to them.

Understanding came only after a quest for the knowledge learned from veterinarians, scientists and physicians. The despair created by this lack of knowledge established a lifelong commitment in him to training the Euthanasia Technician.

Fakkema taught his first euthanasia-by-injection workshop in 1973. Since then, he has conducted technical workshops for animal care and control agencies across the country. He has also served as operations supervisor at Multhomah County Animal Control in Portland and Executive Director of the Santa Cruz, California, SPCA.

With proper knowledge of the physical aspect of euthanasia, Fakkema believes ETs can perform the euthanasia process more efficiently and better handle the emotional stress.

Proper ET training must include a thorough grounding in anatomy, physiology, venipuncture, use of anesthetics, tranquilizers and sedatives, humane restraint, verification of death, employee safety and euthanasia room furnishing.

In 1982, he was asked to serve on the faculty of the American Humane Association's Leadership Management Training Program. In 1987, he received the Rosemary Ames Award and was honored for excellence in teaching at AHA sponsored training programs and outstanding promotion of humane philosophy and objectives.

"How ironic," he muses, "that we 'animal people' must as a part of our job kill animals. Even more ironic is that the technicians performing this crucial function lack proper training."

Most agencies want to provide painless deaths to unwanted animals, yet too many facilities do not know how to achieve this goal.

For the past few years, Fakkema has conducted euthanasia training workshops, and provided crisis intervention on euthanasia at animal care facilities across the country.

While he was in Portland, Fakkema helped write and lobby for legislation to develop uniform euthanasia technician standards. To that end, Oregon was the first state to develop the nation's first statewide training and certification program for euthanasia technicians. Right now he is working with AHA and HSUS to draft policy and procedures on euthanasia guidelines to be used by shelters throughout the country. The definitive document should be published by late 1993.

"Consistency is the key to euthanasia guidelines," says Fakkema. "So that shelters will have access to this information and get the proper procedures in place. The next step is to go state-by-state to get euthanasia procedure and certification laws passed. It will be a struggle in some areas, easy in other states."

Based on his personal experience and in talking with hundreds of ACOs, ETs and shelter staff members over the years, he says some of the biggest euthanasia stressors are not knowing if they are doing it properly; not understanding what they are doing and; wondering what the animal feels.

ETs tell him that other emotional stressors are having to choose which animal has to die; having to euthanize healthy animals and having to euthanize kittens and puppies.

Certain types of animals are more difficult for some people to euthanize. They may be reminded of childhood pets.

Push the Green Button and Walk Away

For those who euthanize animals in chambers, there's a different kind of euthanasia stress.

Euthanasia

Back in 1971, the high altitude decompression chamber was the main euthanasia of choice.

"It was death," recalls Fakkema, "But it wasn't 'good death,' as the Greeks called it. Clearly, it is not a humane method and is now condemned by everybody." But in those days, it was thought to be humane.

"Certain ETs out there, for whatever reasons, seem to think they need to distance themselves from the death process," he said. "In other words, they just want to push the green button and walk away."

(Most of these chambers have a green button that says "start" on them.)

Fakkema said he was very bothered by pushing that green button and walking away.

"Once I understood more clearly what I was doing, I came to realize that comparing that with the more hands-on method of injection and the impact on the animal, the injection method was easier on me than using the chamber," he says.

Fakkema has seen many managers of animal care and control agencies over the years who have supported chambers based on the premise that they don't want their employees to be run through the emotional wringer of having to hold these animals while they die.

This notion comes from people who don't euthanize, he says. It comes from the folks who think they understand it, but they don't. Because in reality, it is easier on a person emotionally to hold the animal and complete the death process with the animal, rather than pushing the green button and walking away.

Others feel like that really bothers them, that they need to be involved in the death process.

Society in general, without thinking about it, believes most people think that it must be easier on the human being to push a button and not be directly involved.

"It is an interesting issue," he says. "A lot of shelters continue to use chambers and they use them with that in mind. For example, a county risk assessment department will say they don't want their employees using hands-on injections because it's too stressful for them. And they've convinced their employees of that."

Over the years, Fakkema has worked with shelters converting from chambers to injection. "There's a tremendous amount of fear, anxiety, resentment and so forth from the staff. They think, 'here's this guy trying to make things more difficult for us,' but after the transition is complete, they realize it is actually much more easier for them."

Because of the disassociation and removal from the death process, the potential for misuse of chambers is much higher.

Like the stories of contests of how many dogs or cats a shelter worker can stuff in a chamber.

"I hear that story everywhere I go," Fakkema says, sadly. "When you push the button and walk away, you not only separate yourself from the process, but also from thinking or caring about overloading it."

Misuse of Injection Method

The biggest misuse of injection is when the ET is not properly trained, uses improper amounts, or tries the wrong route of administration. Some places continue to use intracardiac administration, which goes directly into the heart and is very painful for the animal. That method has been condemned by the American Veterinary Medical Association, HSUS and AHA.

Another misuse is the handling of cats, where a cat is stretched out and squashed down on a table while it is injected. That creates a struggle that challenges the animal's fight or flight systems.

"That is done more than I care to think about," says Fakkema.

Because of the potential for abuse with any method of euthanasia, it's a necessity that the agency staff be properly trained. From the animal's viewpoint, injection can be worse than the chamber. Tranquilizing the animal helps, but overdoing that can have ill effects. It can make the sodium pentobarbital work slower.

There are different kinds of tranquilizers, sedatives, anesthetics, analgesics and so forth. There are different uses on different kinds of animals.

Putting the animal in a dark and quiet place after administering the drugs is important.

Reverence for the animal after euthanasia is important, too. "My recommendation is that animals be treated dead or alive with respect," says Fakkema. "The same way you would treat your own pet."

For example, don't throw the animal's body around after death. "It suggests to me, there is some kind of distancing process going on, that isn't good," says Fakkema. Treat the animal gently."

That is a people issue that is important to the emotional state of the worker. "When I see someone treating animals like that, I believe their emotional time bomb is close to going off," says Fakkema. "At that point, as an administrator or supervisor, I would talk to that individual and ask that person why are they treating animals like that. I would then tell them the kind of behavior I expect."

That kind of behavior could be prompted by a nonanimal problem, be it personal or whatever. It might be helpful for that person to get some counseling.

One of the worst case situations ET's can find themselves in, is to work for directors, managers or boards that distance themselves as far as they can get from euthanasia. They are probably pretty stressed out and overworked themselves. But that doesn't help your situation. Look for support elsewhere.

Besides bosses, thoughtless comments by co-workers can add even more to an ET's stress load.

Dealing With Co-Workers

"Regardless of your job description at the animal shelter—whether you're a licensing clerk, a supervisor or whatever—if you work for an organization that euthanizes animals, then you are part of the euthanasia process. Somewhere along the line, I think it's part of the employee's responsibility to understand how the euthanasia system works. They should not only observe it, but also should have minimal training to understand what goes on," he says. "And they should make sure everybody gets some hands-on training even if they work in front. That would be my solution for it."

A non-ET co-worker might think making a comment like, "no, not that one, he/she was one of my favorites" is purely innocent. But that type of comment is considered *anything* but innocent on the receiving end.

"That can be devastating to an ET. It can be one of those

comments that is remembered for that person's whole career and a huge resentment gets generated," says Fakkema. "You don't expect the public to understand, you don't even expect your family to understand; but you sure as hell expect your co-workers to understand." Fakkema says he has a firm policy that no comments should be made by noneuthanasia staff to ETs about an individual animal. In other words, co-workers should realize the importance of keeping their mouths shut.

How to Deal With the Guilt

You are doing society's dirty work. You must recognize that the public is bringing not only their puppies and kittens, but also their guilt. They want to leave the whole package. You have to accept the puppies and kittens, the dogs, the cats. But you don't have to accept the guilt. It's important to separate the two. It helps to talk with the people who understand this conflict.

Advice from Doug Fakkema:
Euthanasia Consultant and Humane Educator

Don't expect a lot of support on the family or friend level. Get a group of co-workers you can meet with, either on a formal or informal level and talk about what bothers you. That could mean a regularly scheduled support meeting. Or it can be done with unofficial meetings like picnics, volleyball tournaments, softball games and other ways for people to socialize with each other. Find a place to unload some of the stuff you can't unload anywhere else. Do not leave things to chance. The staff should be told you are probably not going to get support at home, but you will get support at work. It should be discussed.

After work, I recommend that people make a deal with their significant other, spouse, friend, etc. to give each other five minutes of uninterrupted *SYMPATHETIC* listening. Really listen to each other. You don't have to say: "If you hate your job so much, just quit." Or try to fix it or feel obligated to offer solutions. Just listen.

Be sure to return the favor and give them five minutes of listening. This will help in terms of getting needs met in a simple manner.

Comments from Bill Hurt Smith
HSUS Animal Control Academy, Tuscaloosa, Alabama

Bill Hurt Smith directs workshops designed to provide support for the Euthanasia Technician and other shelter staff in coping with euthanasia. The workshops examine the attitudes, concerns and feelings of both shelter personnel and the public.

Smith is considered by many to be a pioneer (he dislikes the word "expert") on euthanasia stress.

"Our thrust is to help people deal with their frustrations," he says. "The temptation is to say we're not going to take it anymore, but you can't change the mind of the public. You can't influence the public who does not realize they are responsible for what's going one. You can't say, 'look here, buddy, we're not taking this anymore,' because that's almost like saying you're the dumb person, not me. You can't talk to someone that way and hope to change them in a positive way."

The D Zone

Euthanasia Technicians operate in a "zone of understanding" that Smith calls the "D Zone" for "disquieted." He believes that everyone has the potential for being OK with euthanasia, but it requires an honest look at euthanasia and that individual's feelings towards euthanasia. Like Fakkema, he believes that euthanasia should be part of a shelter's orientation process and preferably should be performed or at least observed by the entire staff, including volunteers, office staff and board of directors.

In his workshops, Euthanasia Technicians are encouraged to talk about their feelings. "We want them to realize that they do have to put those frustrations somewhere but not on the people who we need most to understand, so that we can make some changes."

The real problem with this, he says, is we get frustrated because we have to kill animals. And yet we get blamed for killing animals, like somehow or other it's our fault that these animals have to die. Not the fault of the people who abandon or bring the animals in. He says it's human nature to blame the other person or worse yet, blame themselves. "This was your doing, not mine," he says. "We have to help people understand where to put this anger and how to turn it around."

Attitude Is Important

"Say it straight or you'll show it crooked," says Smith. In other words, if you are forcing yourself to be nice to the public and you'd rather be shouting: 'I'm mad as hell and I'm not going to take it anymore!' there is going to be a problem."

Recognize how to communicate positively, not offensively, to educate the public. It's more important that we help the public understand the situation rather than trying to make them feel bad. Some euthanasia technicians feel that 'if the public felt as bad as I do about this, then they would stop all this unnecessary breeding.'

That is true, he says, but they can't ever feel as bad as the bad we feel. There's no way they can understand it from our perspective unless they walk in our shoes.

Mainly because the public has no concept or understanding whatsoever of the sheer numbers of animals brought into shelters, says Smith. And the public has no concept of what it's like to see euthanasia on a daily basis.

Don't judge the people who bring in animals for surrender. Try to educate them. Put something in their hands. Otherwise, they'll look for any excuse to dump their guilt, along with the unwanted animals and run.

The shelter is their last resort.

The important thing is for ETs and shelter workers to get to a point to realize that the public puts the "guilt business" on your shoulders. It's not your fault or responsibility, so don't take it.

Smith recommends, instead, being polite, but don't try to fake niceness. Comments like: "I wish every story had a happy ending, but it probably won't. You're upset about that and I'm glad to see that," or "Thank you for noticing I'm upset. Not many people ask. Please tell your friends about us and the problems we encounter" should have a better effect.

There are many benefits of attending a Euthanasia Stress workshop. First, technicians get to vent their frustrations. Next, they realize everybody in the room has similar feelings. "I try to guide them into looking into their own feelings, even try to get them somewhat emotional about it, because to deny there is some pain there can be damaging to the technician." The ETs get to recognize which feelings legitimately are their own and which feelings are not their fault or their responsibility.

The Animal Rescue League of Boston, Massachusetts:

An employee "Action Team" was formed to develop humane, equitable and realistic criteria for the selection of animals for euthanasia. First of all, the group based their guidelines for the benefit of the animals entrusted in their care. "Developing the criteria was not an easy task," states the report. It required a lot of tough decisions and a realistic attitude.

"Everyone who loves and cares for animals has a difficult time with the issue of euthanasia and the members of this team are no different," continues the report.

The criteria was based on two options only: Is the animal adoptable or should it be euthanized? Considerations for euthanasia included age of the animal, feral, health, pregnancy, behavior problems and other categories.

The benefit of having specific guidelines is that those animals put up for adoption will be of a quality that adopters deserve from an organization of ARL's professional reputation.

Copies are available free from the League.
Write to:

"Criteria for Selection of Animals for Euthanasia"
Animal Rescue League of Boston

Tom White
Director of Operations
P.O. Box 265
Boston, MA 02117.

Phil Arkow
Education and Publicity Director, Humane Society of the Pikes Peak Region, Colorado Springs, Colorado

"One of the best ways to deal with death is to get a life," says Arkow, who conducts training workshops for animal care and control personnel on dealing with euthanasia stress.

People who do this (ACO or ET) for a living, need to find some other sort of outlet. Get something else going for your spare time.

On the Job:

Take a rational approach. The main problem is for people to find an appropriate mix between compassion and detachment. A rational approach helps to deal with the human emotions. That is, if the right side of the brain can be overridden by the left side of the brain, it can help you survive your job a little bit better. Develop, define and articulate your personal moral principle.

The shelter person is hit from all sides: by the animal rights' crowd who says we shouldn't kill any animal at all; by other people who say we should kill them all. The people who say, 'why did you pick up my dog, but not the dog that was causing the problem?' The people who cause the problem are the ones who make the loudest noise about the solution. The people who really count, know what you are doing and respect you for it. But it's easy to assume that everyone is negative, because they're the only ones you hear from. The fact is, there are people in authority and control who respect what you do. That includes the government people who may be paying your pay check, the donors who may be supporting your organization and the news media.

Suggested Coping Mechanisms:
- Off the job, get involved in something physical like exercise.
- Take time off, you deserve a vacation!
- Get a hobby.
- Visit other shelters. It helps you realize you are not alone.
- Go to workshops and conventions.

And finally, realize, it could be worse. Arkow says his role model is cop Frank Furillo of Hill Street Blues. "If he can handle a day there, anything that goes on here at the shelter can't be that bad."

Or, if you think you've got it bad, visit a meat-packing plant or an abortion clinic, he suggests.

Psychologically, it helps to recognize what actually is the problem: It is the inability for people to make lifelong commitments anymore and when the animal has a behavioral problem or the family moves, it's all too easy to trash the pet. We're stuck with a no-deposit/no-return dog. It's not just spaying and neutering, that's too simplistic a solution. The real fault is the turnover of animals that get dumped in the country or wind up at shelters. Recognize that you may be going through burnout for a lot of different reasons. Euthanasia is one small part of it. There are normal and predictable burnout cycles. They seem to be much more prevalent in the caring professions. We've got this horrible moral dilemma in that, the ones who care the most about the animals, are the ones that have to kill them. But it goes along with the territory. Look for stressors in other areas of your life: family, age, health, unresolved issues or other crises.

It's real easy to say, 'I'm burned out on euthanasia,' but that may just be one part of it. But it could be the key issue, too. Recognize you are not alone. We are all in this together. Take a team attitude. You don't have to do it all. Be sure that euthanasia duties are rotated. Recognize that not everyone is suited for the task. Hire people with farm backgrounds who are used to compassion and detachment with livestock.

Your employer should support opportunities for counseling and therapy.

Frequently Asked Questions About Euthanasia:

- Why do I get blamed for doing society's dirty work?

- What are the stressors for people who must perform euthanasia?

- What does the animal feel?

- How do I know if I'm doing it properly?

- Am I going crazy?

- How can I deal with my family and friends when they call me a puppy killer?

- Do I really have to do it?

- Am I a bad person if I can't handle it?

- What is the best way to deal with my feelings?

- How do I account for all the lives I've taken?

Euthanasia consultants answer these and other questions:

Phil Arkow
Education and Publicity Director, Humane Society of the Pikes Peak Region, Colorado Springs, Colorado

Q. Why do I have to do society's dirty work?

A. I tell them several things. As a shelter worker, you've got enough problems without accepting society's responsibility. Society has caused this problem, not you. You can't be responsible for their mistakes. You didn't cause these animals to be born into an overpopulated world. You didn't cause these pets to become a problem or inconvenience.

Q. How do you help them deal with the conflict of loving animals, but having to kill them?

A. I call it compassion with detachment. It's the same skill that has to be used by nurses, doctors, journalists, police and others. You have to be able to care, but be able to let go. It's not easy. It's obviously not for everybody. It truly makes our group of people a special breed.

Q. At your workshops, are you trying to affirm ACOs/ETs?

A. Yes and no. Being able to perform euthanasia tends to make them special and validate what they do and give them a sense of self-esteem. It makes them realize they are more than just a dog catcher. But you don't necessarily want to promote that. It's not exactly the red badge of honor or courage that most people are going to want to look for. I tell them that euthanasia is an important aspect of what they do. It is important and it is something that nobody is really proud of. It's the dirty job that nobody wants to do. In its own way, the people out there that matter, actually respect you for this despite all the hate and anger that other people direct at you. The people who really count recognize what you are doing, they are glad you are doing it for them. These people feel guilty for the fact that it has to get done.

Doug Fakkema
Euthanasia Consultant and Humane Educator

Q. What are the two biggest stressors for ACOs?

A. One is the conflict of loving animals, but having to euthanize them. The other is wondering if they are doing it correctly. Knowing the right way to do it doesn't make it any easier emotionally, but it makes it a little easier to handle and they can offer more to the animal, by doing it right. Based on my experience (22 years), most people can handle it if they are trained properly and get support at work. But that is so much easier said than done.

Euthanasia Technician is one of the lowest positions on the job ladder and gets the least support. Many directors don't have a clue to what goes on in the euthanasia room and they don't want to know. The decision to keep euthanasia a secret or downplay what they do usually comes from the director or the board. But those most affected are the ones on the front line, in the trenches, faced with euthanizing animals all the time.

Q. What does the animal feel? How do I know if I'm doing it properly?

A. Asking that question indicates that you are sensitive to the animal's needs. That is very commendable. The animal deserves the best of care while staying in our shelter. We owe a humane, peaceful death to every animal that is to be euthanized. The act of euthanasia strikes at the heart of our special feelings toward animals. The feelings which are responsible for most of us working in animal protection in the first place. When euthanasia goes wrong, it bothers us. That's why it's so important to know what you're doing. Knowledge is the broom which sweeps clean the cobwebs of mystery and uncertainty surrounding the euthanasia process. Knowledge gives confidence to those of us who euthanize. Knowledge brings comfort.

The book you are reading is not intended as a technical manual. The Resource Guide lists euthanasia consultants and training materials. Once you have a complete understanding of animal physiology and how the various drugs affect the animal's system, then you will know if you are euthanizing properly. The goals of my training workshop are: 1) increase the ET's effectiveness in the delivery of painless death; 2) diminish the ET's anxiety associated with administering sodium pentobarbital; 3) increase the ET's sense of job satisfaction, and, 4) broaden the euthanasia worker's understanding of animals and self. Consistency is the key to euthanasia guidelines. Shelters need to have access to this information so that proper procedures will be in place. That's why the movement to get uniform euthanasia guidelines approved in each state is so important.

Euthanasia

Karen Stickland
Harrison Memorial Animal Hospital, Denver, Colorado
Conducts support groups for Euthanasia Technicians

Q. Am I going crazy?

A. No. You are a normal person experiencing an abnormal situation. Don't expect the situation to make sense. What you do does make a difference. Let's talk about it. See Section 4 for a detailed discussion on feelings and emotions.

Q. Why is Euthanasia Stress so different from other kinds of stress?

A. Many of the symptoms are the same: loss of appetite, inability to sleep well, having nightmares, flashbacks of animals' faces and engaging in self-destructive behaviors. But the thing that makes Euthanasia Stress so different from other kinds of stress is the conflict of wanting to help and save animals, but having to kill animals. And nobody (except other ETs) wants to hear about it. (See the section on Feelings for a thorough description of the stages of grief and dealing with emotions.)

Bill Hurt Smith
HSUS Animal Control Academy, Tuscaloosa, Alabama

Q. How am I going to answer for all of the lives I've taken? What is God going to do to me?

A. Asked many times over, this question seems to haunt many people. It even prompts bad dreams for some. My best answer came when replying to an ACO who had experienced a dream that resulted in much anguish for him. He dreamed that he had died and could not get into heaven because of the great number of animals which he had euthanized. The animals were standing in front of him and blocking the gates of heaven.

I asked him if he had considered that those animals might not be there to block him at all, but to welcome him as a testimony to the suffering he had prevented by releasing them in a merciful manner from their lives. He spoke to me at the end of the day's workshop to thank me for my comments and to say how relieved he was to discover another answer to his troubled thoughts.

If indeed, we have been given dominion over this earth, then we are to be stewards, keepers. Isn't it then, our responsibility to preserve and protect to the best of our ability the land, the air, the sea and the animals?

Diedre Young
Animal Control Officer, Kennel Master and ET, Benton, Arkansas
Conducts euthanasia workshops and operates a euthanasia hotline from her home

Q. How can you do your job, but stay uninvolved?

A. I tell them, don't look the animal in the face. Don't get emotionally involved with the animal. I know it's hard to do. If you do get involved, you'll have to get somebody else to do it.

Q. How can I deal with my family and friends when they call me a puppy killer?

A. It helps to talk to someone about your feelings. But some people don't have anyone to talk to. Some try to talk to their husbands, wives, boyfriends, fathers, mothers, whatever but they don't want to hear about it. It's really hard, especially coming from someone you love.

Mike Burgwin
National Animal Control Association, Indianola, Washington

Q. Do I really have to do it?

A. I equate being an ACO with being a policeman. You can't go out there and be a good policeman and throw up. You may feel like it, but you've got to learn how to control it, because the job doesn't get done if you've over there throwing up. The ACOs that have learned to handle it are very technical. They want to make sure they are doing it correctly and only have to do it once. That way it's minimum stress on the animal. The animals have feelings and know from the feeling of your own hands, what your muscles are doing.

Q. What if I can't handle it?

A. There are those individuals who should never be doing this job. That doesn't make you a bad person. That just means this is not your kind of work. Don't feel like a failure. People have to look at what they feel comfortable doing because then they'll do their job better.

Q. Is there something wrong with me because I can't do it?

A. No. There is something wrong with you if you insist on trying and you can't do it. Now the animal is going to suffer; plus you won't carry your share of the load. Somebody else will have to do your duties. It's not just that you're forcing yourself to do something you don't like, the ripple effect is also harmful to the animal and the staff. Do something you're comfortable with. That's all we're saying. The business itself is stressful.

Dennis Fetko, Ph.D., "Dr. Dog"
Applied Animal Behaviorist, San Diego, California

Q. In private practice, the most common question I hear is, "How do I know it's time?" But in the shelter, the most common question is, "how do I make the determination of adopting or euthanizing?"

A. If an ACO, Humane Officer or Euthanasia Technician sees a dog acting unfriendly, he or she may assume asocial or antisocial behavior is the norm for that animal in that situation. If you are not making threatening gestures or causing pain, ask yourself: 'Why is a domestic pet being snotty to me?' If you, an experienced officer and handler, are having a problem with that dog, how do you expect someone with only a fraction of your experience to be able to handle that dog and succeed with it? Realize your own competence. You are somebody who handles strange dogs of all different sizes and genders, and dogs that have received all kinds of treatment. They have been actively abused, dumped and neglected, loved to death and spoiled rotten. If you handle those dogs, 40 hours a week, 50 weeks a year, YOU are the expert. You are a thousand times more competent at handling dogs than the person looking to adopt one, so if you had trouble with it for no apparent reason, how dare you give it up for adoption.

Euthanasia

Q. People blame me for doing this. How do I respond?

A. If you think death is the worst thing that will happen to an animal, I envy you. After all you've been through in the animal world, especially if you've worked full time for several years, you've encountered horrible cases of abuse, neglect and animal injury. Whether you want to or not, you will frequently develop the attitude that death is not the worst thing that can happen. You will instead think, 'I love this animal so much, I would rather put it down than have it live five more years of agony, or die on the highway, be bitten by rattlesnakes or become hawk or bobcat food, suffer untreated diseases or starve to death. Unfortunately, to most people that choice is just an intellectual exercise in frustration and only hypothetical. To ACOs, it is part of their daily reality, so your standards are different. Here comes someone who gets into animal control out of love for animals, then they find out they have to chase and sometimes kill them. Oftentimes they do so willingly because they know how horrible some animals' lives are. And then they go to a party and somebody says: 'Oh, a dog catcher! and nearly spits at them like they're lepers. What a price to pay! ACOs suffer this terrible castigation when they are, amazingly enough, among the most humane people around.

Some of the biggest problems of the job don't have to do with animals, but dealing with people. Remember the '60's phrase: 'Suppose they gave a war and nobody came?' How about replying to your accuser: 'Suppose we gave a euthanasia session and the public saw to it that no dogs were available?'

Chris Powell
Shelter Manager, Peninsula Humane Society, San Mateo County, California

Q. What is the best way to deal with my feelings?

A. There's not any one universal way you can deal with it. I don't want people to think there is any one way to deal with Euthanasia Stress. Sometimes what happens in shelters, is that people don't allow people to be individuals. They think, well, we all have to think this way or we all have to feel this way. We don't have to feel any one way but we have to do whatever we can to get the job done. Sometimes I think people who work in shelters are called hard and not caring. I've realized over the years that if people are real hard after working in shelters for a long time, it's not that they are uncaring at all, it's simply the way they've been able to come to terms and they put up this kind of little wall that allows them to do their job. I may look at that and say, that's not right. But it allows this person to come back day after day after day and deal with this situation instead of walking out. It's a defense mechanism.

Q. What do you think about the fact many shelters are telling the public about, even publicizing, euthanasia?

A. I think it's great. I think that for far too long, we (shelters) contributed to our own problem because we hid it from the public, then it got out of hand. The public didn't know what was going on because we didn't let them know what was going on. I think the best thing we can do is not

Euthanasia

hide a single thing. I was in shelters when we didn't tell the public. We used to tell people we don't kill animals, we don't euthanize animals. We created our own situation. We were our own worst enemies in doing that. By not hiding this thing, we also give the staff a sense of pride. Before we were telling them to be ashamed of what they were doing. We told them, "Don't you dare tell the public, but you're not supposed to feel bad." Now we let people deal with their feelings.

Q. What are some ways people can deal with their feelings?

A. Everyone has to deal with Euthanasia Stress in his or her own way. For some people, it is writing their thoughts in a journal. For others, it's going out and playing with the animals in the kennels. For some, it's crying. There's not just one universal answer.

It's important that people have some hope that the situation is getting better. I think if people came into a shelter situation and euthanized on a daily basis and just believed that it wouldn't make one bit of difference, then nobody would stay very long. But the fact is that over the years, people have learned about spay/neutering and in many, many urban shelters the amount of puppies brought into shelters has gone down. And we're now able to work on people to spay/neuter feral cats.

Don't give up hope. You are not alone. You are making a difference.

For People in Wildlife Rehabilitation and Rescue Who are Faced with Euthanasia

Quality of life for injured animals is an issue that rages on and will continue to fester among wildlife rehabilitators and volunteers. Breeding and killing animals such as mice to feed raptors and snakes are other difficult decisions they face.

And rehabilitators are faced with wondering if they are euthanizing animals humanely.

Many animal shelters have their own wildlife center or know individuals, organizations or sanctuaries to call to deal with wildlife. I hate the term 'nuisance wildlife.' We know who the REAL nuisance is: It carries a gun and a six-pack.

"It should be called 'nuisance humans,'" says Nancy Treiber, director of Wildlife Rescue and Sanctuary, Pensacola, Florida. She is often faced with decisions on euthanasia. "We see so much that is caused by humane ignorance. People want me to come get owls out of the trees and turtles out of their yards."

On the other extreme, Treiber has seen people keep severely handicapped wildlife as pets. "I've seen a squirrel with a broken back that has to drag itself around in a cage. To me, that's pitiful. That is something that should never be allowed. An animal that has no dignity, no life. It's cruel," she says. "My decisions to euthanize are never based on what kind of animal it is: whether it is a sparrow, eagle, hawk, wild rabbit or doe. It doesn't matter to me. Each individual animal is important to me. We take them all in and treat them all the same.

"That's because if we only saved all the hawks, we'd run

Euthanasia

out of rabbits. I try to think I'm keeping a balance. There's always going to be an imbalance with human intervention, but it would be even more unbalanced if we euthanized every sparrow."

Euthanasia is a reality of wildlife rescue and rehabilitation. Not surprisingly, euthanasia is a difficult and sensitive subject among wildlife rehabilitators.

"Euthanasia is not supposed to be easy," says Ken Wolff, director of the Raptor Room and the Grounded Eagle Foundation in Montana who calls euthanasia a "medical tool." "You're not supposed to like killing things. I hate killing things. It's unnatural to like it. I'd be real concerned if you do like killing things."

Wolff estimates he takes in about 300 birds a year at the wildlife rehabilitation facility, of which 3 percent to 8 percent have to be euthanized. "Every bird that arrives here for treatment is effectively a dead bird. Every one we can put back in the sky is a bonus bird."

> "If a bird is going to die with or without treatment, put it down. If a bird is obviously not going to fly again, put it down. If a wing must 'come off,' put it down. Broken wing joints will usually call for euthanasia. Exceptions: If you have a particular request for a grounded bird for use in a zoo, education, breeding, research. Save a good specimen for this request. There will never be a shortage of broken birds." *From The Raptor Room Euthanasia Policy/Protocol.*

And the sooner euthanasia is carried out, the easier it is emotionally on the rehabilitator and rescuer.

For example, an owl just came into his center "barely alive" with a bullet in its brain. As soon as he examined it, he knew there was no hope for the bird. "In that case, the kindest thing we can do for that bird is to put it to sleep," he says.

"What is a life in a cage for a bird that was intended to fly?" Wolff asks. "We can't save, feed and care for all the one-winged robins of the world, or the one-winged great horned owls, in particular, common species. If it doesn't serve its population, it doesn't serve a purpose.

"I might treat 40 to 50 great horned owls a year; half or so of them can fly. I don't have enough mice, money, time or energy to care for those that can't fly. I keep a little list of people or facilities who might want something in particular; like an eagle, goshawks or a less than common bird.

"Some of those I can give to people or facilities who may be looking for a particular species. If I don't know of any place for them, then they have to go to sleep," says Wolff.
"It's such a tremendous waste of resources, both human and financial. Resources are always so limited. Those resources could be used to help wildlife be wildlife rather than maintaining a bunch of wild animals in a cage," says Wolff.

"I don't feel it's my job to save injured wildlife just for the sake of saving them. I focus on fixing broken birds," he says. "I can save just about anything, but I haven't done the animals any favors by doing so, if it's not going to be a wild animal again."

Back in Florida, Treiber says she is against keeping a bird in a cage unless it is as close to what the bird is used to in the wild. "A bird that is unhappy, can't adjust and can't exist that way, is better off euthanized. It is almost a favor to them to release them from their suffering. The only birds we keep are the ones that have adjusted to captivity."

Euthanasia

For example, at the sanctuary, there are two handicapped red-tailed hawks who can't survive in the wild. But they have mated for life after they have come into the sanctuary. They stayed together, laid eggs in captivity and raised young. Last year two captive-born redtails were released and now there are three eggs ready to hatch this year. "That's the beauty of it," says Treiber, proudly. "Even though they are crippled and can't go back into the wild, their offspring will. But then again we have redtails that can't adjust, they might have a wing missing or other horrible injuries. Then I do the right thing for them which is euthanasia. It's more of a release for them, but it's not something I enjoy doing."

Tough Call

It's hard to maintain balance between detachment and compassion.

"This is a very real job; a lot of people don't have my attitude and have trouble dealing with it. I wonder if there might be long-term damage to working with these animals. I try not to go to far off the deep end, but if I do, I crawl back up," Wolff says, laughing. "I'm fortunate to live 85 miles from town. I live out where I can be with animals in the wild. I can talk to free wild animals, grizzly bears, owls, eagles, ones I or nobody else has messed with."

Macho Men

It's OK to feel sad. "I'm not saying it's easy. I consider myself your basic male macho type, and I cry when I have to put a bird to sleep," says Wolff. "There aren't many men in this business as a rule and a lot of them have the typical American male problems, which is another sad cause in itself."

Euthanasia hurts the most, Wolff says, when he's invested a great amount of time, emotion and expense with a bird and then realizes it's not going to make it. "That," he says, "really hurts. But we must learn from it and we go on."

The birds that get better makes the tough stuff like euthanasia a little easier to take. "I focus on my releases. The birds that can fly again. That makes all this pretty cool," he says. "If I keep thinking about the birds I couldn't save and I've had to kill over the past 10 or 15 years, I'd go crazy."

Emotional Toll

However you look at it, euthanasia is a stressful task. And depending on the circumstances involved and the situation of the animal, it's far less stressful to euthanize an old, sick, dying animal than a young, healthy animal that has nowhere to go.

That's why loss and grief are major stressors for both companion animal caregivers and wildlife rehabilitators, says Ira Slotkin, an animal loss consultant in Austin, Texas.

But people in wildlife rehabilitation and rescue, whether volunteers or professionals, deal with several different loss issues compared to people who work with companion animals.

"People get more attached to wildlife. They put a tremendous emotional investment in what they do. That's one of the reasons people feel so overwhelmed by euthanasia.

When they euthanize a bird they have been unable to rehabilitate, they can feel like they are destroying a part of the environment they hoped to save. People can be overwhelmed by that." The words "rescue" and "rehabilitation," describe how that person looks at him or herself. If they consider themselves to be a rescuer, then euthanasia makes them a failure. Any kind of loss causes stress and that loss can trigger other losses they have experienced. Obviously, there is the direct loss of that animal. Next there's the loss of confidence in themselves because they had hoped to make a difference in that animal's life. And, in the larger sense of the world and animal life, there's the loss of trying to save the environment. The rescuer and rehabilitator may think: 'I may not be able to save this world, but I can save this turtle, otter or pigeon.' An endangered species is part of an accountable group. It's not an infinite group of kittens and puppies.

For those reasons, both shelters and wildlife centers need employee assistance programs and internal support systems. "They need support all the way around," says Slotkin. "Otherwise they wind up with excessive turnover and employees with substance abuse problems."

Laboratory Technicians and Research Animals

The issue of animals obtained and kept for science and medical research is a highly controversial and an emotionally charged subject both within and outside the laboratory.

Arnold Arluke, professor of sociology and anthropology

at Northeastern University in Boston studied 15 laboratories and research centers with around 400 principal investigators, veterinarians, postdoctoral and graduate students, research technicians and animal caretakers. He is writing a book on the subject.

> "While most people I studied seemed to have come to terms with their use of animals, many had not. Few people had frequent signs of depression or anxiety, such as nightmares, sleep loss, and increased alcohol consumption, that they attributed to working with animals. However, more moderate and episodic feelings of discomfort were common and were expressed as background uneasiness and guilt. About 20 percent of the interviewees, compared animal experimentation, however tentatively, to the Holocaust. Uneasiness was particularly noticeable among newcomers; with seasoned workers, it was most common among animal caretakers.
> *From "Trapped in a guilt cage," by Arnold Arluke, New Scientist, April 1992.*

Within the laboratory, workers will try to avoid having or showing feelings for the animals. Animals are called "models"; their costs are listed under "supplies" in grant proposals and they were given numbers instead of names.

Death is a routine part of laboratory life, but never mentioned. Terms such as "dispatched," "terminated," "cervically dislocated," "exsanguinated," "decapitated" or "put down," while whole rooms were "depopulated" or simply "cleaned," writes Arluke.

Within the scientific hierarchy, technicians and animal caretakers find it harder to treat animals as objects because they have the most direct contact with the animals.

"It was very difficult for me to euthanize," a former research laboratory technician in Washington, D.C., tells me. "That's one of the reasons I left. No one would address the difficulty. They just said, 'deal with it. It's your problem.' "It hurts to have to euthanize, especially the times when something goes wrong. That is when it bothers you the most. The pain, the suffering, the loss," says the former lab tech who did not want to be identified for fear of reaction from animal terrorist groups.

People in research facilities are very misunderstood. They see the benefit of research for animals and humans. Generally it does fall on the veterinarians, caretakers and technicians to deal with euthanasia issues, not the investigators. It's not a pleasant thing. "I was very cautious about telling people what I did. People don't want to hear that you do research on animals. They don't want to hear that you kill animals; it turns people off big time," she says.

And lab animals wind up staying in research facilities for years, much longer than animals in shelters. After the research is over, some animals are placed in sanctuaries. But that's not always the best place for long-term care. Euthanasia is considered the best alternative for the animal.

"I was in research ten years ago and it's changed dramatically. I have to give credit to the animal rights groups that have demanded change. Humane treatment of animals in research facilities is now being addressed better than it's ever been," she says.

"They used to tell us, 'it's just an animal, it's just a number, don't get attached.' But now they are saying to give this animal the best life it can have, even though it may be short. For however long that animal's life may be, make it as humane as possible. In order to present the best research and research data, you must be so attuned to the animals in your facility. Now they say you must care for that animal as if it were your own and be concerned about its physical, emotional and psychological welfare. I had never expected to hear this and these were from top researchers," she says.

But that also puts a lot of stress on technicians who are seeing the animal every day for years and then have to euthanize it.

As with all of us who are faced with difficult decisions about animals, the research community is wrestling with these issues and finding out there is no one solution or way to deal with it.

The Euthanasia Room

- Repaint the euthanasia room so it's a bright color.

- Control the odors; keep it clean.

- Have pleasant, soft background music playing.

- Put a blanket over the cage, so the animal is kept quiet.

- Treat the animal with respect, even after it is dead.

- Bag the animal to provide a little more detachment.

- Keep a journal in the room for people to write down their comments, feelings. Discuss these comments in a safe group setting.

These are simple suggestions, but they can be very effective. Remember: There is no one way. Find what is comfortable to you and what meets your needs.

Suggestions for Co-workers Who *Don't* Have to Euthanize Animals

—submitted by the Tri-Lakes Animal Shelter, New York

- Don't question those who do. It only makes their job more difficult.
- Staff members who are not involved in euthanasia duties are expected to respect the feelings of those who do.
- Disparaging comments are extremely detrimental, both to the morale of the staff and to the reputation of the shelter.
- The general public may greatly misunderstand the cause and need for euthanasia in animal holding facilities.
- To discredit any facility because euthanasia is performed there, may lead some persons to abandon or otherwise indiscriminately dispose of unwanted animals.
- Tremendous suffering is most often the fate of abandoned pets. This is also true of animals placed in the homes of irresponsible individuals.
- Therefore a great disservice to all animal welfare organizations whose focus is to provide a refuge for unwanted animals while helping the public understand that the most responsible and effective way to diminish the need for euthanasia is to prevent the overpopulation of companion animals through spaying and neutering.
- It is hoped that all staff members will frankly discuss their feelings and attitudes about euthanasia with each other. Euthanasia is a profoundly stressful but necessary reality of shelter work.

If You Volunteer at a Shelter

Euthanasia is a very difficult subject to cope with. Unfortunately, due to the insurmountable number of animals brought into shelters, there is no choice but to euthanize. Injury, severe illness, behavioral problems and at times a sheer lack of space all contribute to a need for euthanasia. It is something for you to think about before making a commitment to volunteer at the shelter. You may arrive one day to walk your "favorite" dog only to find he is being led out to be euthanized. This can be very emotional. This isn't a scare tactic to keep you away, it is a fact you need to be aware of. Your ability to accept and deal with this needs to be addressed. Each decision to euthanize for each and every animal is well thought through.

Frequently asked questions from volunteers about euthanasia:

- Why are you doing this?
- How can you kill them? You people are so cold-hearted.

We become attached to the animals too, but the facts are: for every dog or cat that gets adopted, there are two to three others waiting. Decisions, however unpopular, must be made. Please encourage spaying and neutering to fight pet overpopulation.

Euthanasia

Summary

- Be skilled. Know what you're doing. Get training and certification. Go to workshops. Stay up on research. When in doubt, ask questions!
- Realize your own competence. Trust your judgment. Believe in your own instincts.
- You may accept society's unwanted animals, but don't accept their guilt.
- Take the opportunity to educate the public. Don't leave a person as ignorant as you found them. Tell people the right and wrong things to do to animals.
- Don't accept the blame from the public, your family, friends or co-workers.
- Don't give up hope. You are not alone. You are making a difference.
- Keep a journal in the euthanasia room. It can be unsigned or signed. Encourage the entire staff to contribute to it.
- Find someone you trust and feel safe with about sharing your feelings.
- Don't minimize your situation. "We *only* do 2,000 dogs a year. *They* have to euthanize 10,000 dogs a year." Everybody's situation is unique and has its own set of stressors and problems.

Be kind to yourself!

Paws for Thought: Where do you stand on euthanasia? Take the time to examine your feelings about it. Write about it.

Section 3:
Voices: Us and Them

Voices: Us and Them
Is anybody listening to the Unsung Heroes in the Hood?

We're the people who scoop the poop, clean the pens and put the animals to sleep—forever. We're expected to deal with angry, ignorant members of our community.

The following comments were made by a cross-section of "Us" people who talked about animals, people and euthanasia.

Can you relate to any of this?

By the way, "*Them*" get a chance to speak at the end of this chapter.

Us:

From a Euthanasia Technician/kennel keeper/licensing clerk and fill-in for other chores at the shelter:
"It's like go kill a dog and now be nice to these people. That's the worst part for me. You've got 10 or 15 animals that have got to go, but wait a minute. We need help in the office, do this first. It's real hard. I can do one or the other, but don't ask me to do both. And my boss said I'm getting real snotty with these people."

From Lois Kopecky of Iowa:
"As Euthanasia Technicians, we recognize that we work with animals because we love them. But let's be honest, we end up having to kill them. Therefore, we must be the best we can be."

From an ET in Mississippi:
"I don't like to do euthanasia, but if I quit, they'll probably put some real jerk in here to do it. At least I care about the animals."

From an ET in Virginia:
"Do you remember the first time? Can you not forget the last time? Even if you say, 'it doesn't bother me,' you know exactly how many animals it's been."

From a shelter volunteer and former lab tech:
"We must help the animals. The animals can't help themselves, they can't control their populations. It doesn't matter where we go in the world. We have altered so many things, we can't be hands off now. If we could, that would be wonderful but even in the national park system we have manipulated it so much. We've gotten ourselves in a situation we can't stop."

From Venaye Reese, D.V.M. field veterinarian, Clemson University in South Carolina:
"In many cases, it's a blessing to control the final circumstances of saying good-bye, especially with larger animals. You can choose a sunny day and provide the final time compared to 2 a.m. and the animal is in a ditch in the mud. I deal with animals dying all the time. The majority don't

get to die well; they are abandoned; they are hurt, sick, diseased. They die not the best death. We're trying to give them the very best we can give them. We can't be perfect.

"I don't want people to feel so guilty if they cause a moment of pain or anxiety. It's important to have some perspective that this is much better than the way the majority of animals get to die. This gives ETs support they generally don't get..."

From Bill Smith, euthanasia consultant:
"We can throw the guilt away pretty easy. We must deal with the sorrow and stress. If we don't, it will deal with us!"

Dr. Reese continues:
"The how, when and where to deal with euthanasia is based on the comfort of the animal and not on one's own feelings. Go beyond yourselves. Be considerate of the animal first.

"At shelters, be clear about the decision-making part. The real responsibility falls on society, not the shelters. That's a public education aspect we need to work on.

"When considering the method of handling and euthanasia, be sure to consider all aspects of the species and the individual animal involved: age, size, temperament, tameness, nocturnal, diurnal habits, and so forth. All of these should be considered and the best judgment used. Many people will say we just do it this way. You have to be flexible."

"I get very upset thinking about the pure animal rights and medical research field. That type of total antagonism is damaging for both sides. I think we should be striving for educating everyone who deals with animals in stressful ways, handling, or any form of euthanasia to do it as humanely as possible."

From Karen Stickland, ET support group coordinator in Colorado:
"If you ask any shelter director what his or her biggest problems are, euthanasia is going to be one of the top two items. Budget is going to be the other big problem."

Nan Weitzman of the Responsible Dog Owners Association in Pennsylvania:
"There's such a small minority of people that abuses animals. The biggest majority of people are just plain ignorant. A lot of people don't realize a dog is not born automatically trained. I call it the Lassie Syndrome.

"People have this concept. They see these dogs on television. If it's a collie they think it's just like Lassie. They expect it to know automatically to sit, heel, come, stay, not go to the bathroom on the floor and not eat the sofa.

"People think their dogs think like humans. The guy up the street told me he was surprised that his dog got hit by a car. He says 'I thought my dog had an IQ of 180 and understood the concept that if you run in front of car, you'll die.'

"My whole objective is to work with the community. Let's get people educated. Educate them and they will get their dogs spayed and neutered. And teach them that dogs are not born automatically trained."

From an elementary teacher and shelter volunteer in California:
"One of the things that is good about humane education with children is using the peer pressure of the child to educate the parent."

From a retired veterinarian in Iowa:
"Patience is the key, after the animal is put to sleep, I like for the ET to say: 'That wasn't too bad.'"

From a pharmaceutical manufacturer of euthanasia drugs:
"Euthanasia is a tough job, but you have to face up to it."

From a shelter director in a rural part of Massachusetts:
"I still look for the good in people at surrender time. But I feel sad and angry about euthanasia. I also feel proud that I am helping the animals and relieving their suffering."

Ken Wolff, director of the Raptor Room, Montana:
"Sometimes, sadly enough, death is the best thing for the animal. Most of the cases I get around here, the bird is so badly damaged, I look at it as alleviating pain, so that makes it easier. We can't save all the broken robins of the world. But it is never easy. We must concentrate on what's best for the animal. We must talk about euthanasia in real terms. That helps the animals more. That's the bottom line. We sometimes save broken robins for human reasons. Humans and human feelings and emotions have to take a back seat behind what's best for the animal."

Voices

From a shelter director in a rural part of Florida:
"It don't bother me to do euthanasia. I've done over 6,000 animals. I just wish I didn't have to do it behind the barn."

From Carter Luke, MSPCA, Boston:
"When people say, 'I couldn't do your job,' shelter people and ETs perceive that statement to mean, "I'm too sensitive and too caring to do that. You must not be caring and sensitive in order do that job.' I think that's why a lot of shelter people react negatively to that type of comment. The reality is, most people don't mean it that way, but that certainly is the way most shelter people take it."

From the Trenches:

Orangeburg, South Carolina, Times and Democrat front page headline:
" 'Puppy Mill' case ends with $14,000 in fines paid to county"

Henry Brzezinski, executive director, Columbia, South Carolina Humane SPCA:
"I believe euthanasia should be a shared duty."

Rob Lee, director, John Ancrum SPCA, Charleston, South Carolina area:
"As long as euthanasia is such a large part of our daily responsibilities, there is no acceptable excuse for us to continue to allow fertile animals to leave this shelter through the front door while truckloads of dead ones are

71

being taken out the back door. There is an obligation to provide more than a merciful death for unwanted animals."

From Doug Fakkema, euthanasia consultant:
"You don't put cats and dogs to sleep. You put them to death because they don't wake up."

Front a counter clerk at an animal shelter in Florida:
"Finding a good home is the goal. Dead is not the worst thing that can happen to an animal. Just what is a good home?"

Phil Arkow, Humane Society of the Pikes Peak Region, Colorado Springs, Colorado:
"I see us in this field as urban game wardens. What we are doing, unfortunately, is culling a certain population of animals—about four percent, as it turns out, so the rest can survive on limited resources. That's a technical or abstract way of looking at it. Obviously there is an emotional factor with every one of these deaths. But you can look at it this way and I know this is not going to be popular. But this is similar to hunting. I am not a hunter. I do not approve of hunting, but those people who do hunt justify it as a population control device. What euthanasia technicians are doing, are making sure the population control is done painlessly and humanely."

From a college student and shelter volunteer in New Mexico:
"When will this suffering end?"

Voices

From a National Animal Control Association Editorial:
"You are caught between the animal rights extremists and animal trappers."

In California:
"Our board and our staff decided we would go for it and invite the press into the euthanasia room," says Tricia Gallegos, director of Development and Public Affairs at the Peninsula Humane Society, California. "Internally, we were very organized and orchestrated. We tried to be honest with everything we did."

In the State of Washington:
The Responsible Breeding Ordinance is now law and is considered the toughest of its kind in the nation. The ordinance requires that all dogs and cats older than six months be spayed or neutered unless an unaltered animal license has been obtained. No animal over the age of six months can be released from a shelter without being altered.

Tim Greyhavens, executive director of Progressive Animal Welfare Society said the law is working because the numbers of animals euthanized during 1991 "dropped drastically."

"I would urge everybody not to waste any more time," says Greyhavens. "Do something right away. We've waited long enough. Anything that is done, is going to be better than to continue the killing."

In Texas:
After Austin changed the definition of pet ownership to "if you feed it, you own it," retired Executive Director of

the Humane Society of Austin and Travis County, Texas, Doyle Nordyke said the first few people who called in "gave us a hard time and said 'all you people at the Humane Society want to do is kill, kill, kill.' We tried to explain to them, that we're trying to get people to be more responsible."

Truth in Advertising

From a public service ad campaign in Austin, Texas:
"If you thought teaching your kids about sex was difficult...try teaching your pets."

From an American Humane Association public service ad:
"Who Says Neutered Dogs Have No Balls?"

From a Pet Overpopulation brochure, Humane Society, Missoula, Montana:
"You may believe in the new sexual freedom...but don't lay it on your pets!"

People Are Watching Us

From David H. Schroeder, Ph.D., who wrote the article, "Animal Control Workers: Ordinary People, Extraordinary Stress":
"I don't know why people stay at these jobs. Maybe you should do a survey on it."

From the sociological study, "Animals, Attitudes, and Anthropomorphic Sentiment: The Social Construction

of Meat and Fur in Post-Industrial Society," by C. Eddie Palmer and Craig J. Forsyth, 1992:
"As post industrialization increases, people will become further and further removed from first-hand experience with the food chains...One result is the current wave of interest in animal welfare and animal rights."

Them:

"How did my dog get pregnant?"

"You will find a good home for my _____(fill in the blank: unwanted litter of puppies, kittens) The mother (cat, dog) just keeps getting pregnant."

"I don't want this dog anymore. He doesn't match my new furniture."

"I can't keep this cat. It kicks the litter out of its box."

"I have to have the latest _____." (potbellied pig, snake, lizard or designer dog) fad pet.

"Best dog I ever had." (reason for surrender statement)

From an animal rights activist in California:
"PETA gets to the bottom line. That is how it should be. And it's very good at getting the attention of the media."

Radio personality Rush Limbaugh:
"Animals have no rights."

Us vs. Them:
A cat and 166 dogs were confiscated by the Columbia South Carolina Humane Society. Many of the dogs had

pneumonia, internal parasites and jaw damage. The puppy mill operator's comments after the raid:

"I'll admit this wasn't the Buckingham Palace for the dogs, but couldn't they (the Humane Society) come in and say, 'This isn't acceptable, could you clean it up please?' They just came in like Nazis hunting the Jews."

Comments by county prosecutor after dogs were returned to the owner: "This is the same thing as giving drugs back to a drug dealer and asking him to hold them until trial so I can prove my case."

From the "Isn't pet overpopulation cute?" department, a cartoon in *Reader's Digest*:

A mother cat complaining to another mother cat: "56 kittens and not one of them ever calls me."

From the late Anthropologist Margaret Mead:

"Never doubt that a small group of thoughtful, committed citizens can change the world; indeed, it's the only thing that ever has."

Don't give up hope.

Section 4:
Feelings, Emotions

Feelings, Emotions

"I got lost on the Human Highway." — Neil Young.
What about the humane highway? Are you stuck?

"People having to kill animals they are hired to take care of. It's a conflict that is not present anywhere else. If we're not OK, we can't do any good for the animals."— Karen Stickland

"Animal care workers have one of the toughest and most unique jobs in existence. They must love and respect animals, and hold them in the highest regard. They must euthanize healthy animals, and provide those animals the most secure and friendly atmosphere possible while doing so. They must rationalize euthanasia as being the best thing for the animals and being part of the overall solution. Then they must face the people who are the cause of the mass euthanasia. They must deal with them professionally and tactfully, and they must utilize that contact to attempt to educate the public." —Doug Kelly

Karen Stickland and Doug Kelly help organize and lead support groups for Euthanasia Technicians in Colorado.

Feelings, Emotions

Here are some of their suggestions and comments about dealing with feelings and emotions.

Karen says, "I'll be the first person to admit that FEELINGS are scary, especially sad FEELINGS. But for some of us, it's even hard to feel happy, especially when we are emotionally numbed because of stressful circumstances (like euthanasia). Shutting down is a survival mechanism. You may say it doesn't bother you, but in some way it does. A way that's totally individual to you.

There will never be neat and tidy ways to deal with animal issues such as abandonment, abuse, neglect and the fact that there are simply too many animals that need good homes. Part of the trauma surrounding the killing of animals deals directly with these conflicts and how you decide to resolve them. The conflicts and their resolutions go on day after day, with no real end in sight.

When you entered the animal welfare field, you believed strongly that you could and would make a difference. That was the driving force, along with your love of animals that brought you here in the first place. Why do you now find yourself feeling helpless and almost victimized by your own compassion and love for animals? It's time to tell the truth: The truth is that you are in a unique way victimized by your compassion.

Even if you think you're totally OK, that it's everyone else around you who is so messed up, just for a moment acknowledge, admit that there is a conflict. Awareness is the beginning of the journey.

You Are Not Alone.

You Will Survive This Conflict.

As victim assistance counselors and former ETs Karen Stickland and Doug Kelly see similarities between what ETs and ACOs experience and what police officers and victims of violent crimes experience. In confidential support groups, they help ETs deal with feelings of loss and grief. They tell them what they can expect to experience.

Depending on how long you have been involved in the killing of animals, you are very likely experiencing long-term grief. The feelings are very similar to those people who experience Post Traumatic Stress Disorder (PTSD). Recurring Euthanasia Stress Syndrome (RESS) is a term for normal people dealing with abnormal circumstances. Like you.

The losses you suffer each day are real and cumulative. Because they build on each other day after day, your ability to resolve each one in time to go on to the next animal is impaired. It is perfectly natural and expected that you feel hopeless about whether you will ever be able to feel better emotionally and able to return to enjoying a sense of accomplishment on your job. That's why it is important to talk with others in the same situation.

Karen and Doug recommend that ACOs and ETs see a physician for a physical check-up and let the doctor know what kind of stress they're going through. The doctor may have some suggestions for a healthy diet designed to provide the proper nourishment, appropriate exercise and ways to make sure that they are taking care of themselves. "Put some real effort into taking good care of yourself. You are definitely worth it!" they say.

You lose a little bit of yourself, every time you deny yourself pride and a sense of accomplishment in your job. When outsiders or civilians ask what you do for a living, do you hesitate to tell them the truth and give them a generic description of your job?

The truth is that you work with animals because you love them, and you give this to the animals because your heart and soul is in it.

Both the animals and their owners are fortunate that you are involved in this profession. Learn to take pride in your dedication to your chosen field.

It's normal to feel loss when you must kill animals, but the feelings of loss intensify when you can't talk to anyone about it.

It may be unrealistic to depend solely on your friends for the understanding and support you need.. Often the only people who can hear about it are other ACOs and ETs. That's what a support group is all about. We'll be here for each other, we can take care of each other, it's really OK.

Times Are Changing

It used to be a rule of thumb in shelters of the past, that if euthanasia bothered you then you couldn't do the job. Now we have recognized that it's important to care about the animals and that killing them will be difficult because we care. We are starting to see the human tragedy of it instead of solely focusing on the animal tragedy part of it.

Animal lovers chose this profession because they wanted to take care of animals, but after a day or two on the job, they are asked to kill animals. This doesn't make any sense but they keep going back. They want to believe that they can make a difference and that the situation will improve but are continually faced with the conflict.

The minute we forget that human beings are more important than animals, we haven't taken care of ourselves.
The animals will be worse off if we burn out.
The animals KNOW you make a difference.
ACOs, ETs and shelter workers make a big difference. In many cases, the only real care an animal has ever received is at a shelter.

Whether they are there for two days or two weeks, the animal who is saved from traffic, injury, disease and neglect and is either returned to its owner, adopted to a good home or humanely euthanized knows you make a difference. Have you ever considered how things would be if caring, rational people weren't providing these services?

Let's Talk About Grief

Stick your big toe in the ocean of emotions. Test the waters. Denial is not a river in Egypt.

Author Barbara Lazear Ascher wrote about grief brought on by her brother's death in "Landscape Without Gravity: A Memoir of Grief."(Delphinium Books, 1993).

"Grief is such a soup. And to separate guilt from the rage and sorrow, I don't know if I can."

Ascher's advice to anyone suffering as she did is to: "Talk. Talk. Talk. Find people to talk to. And absolutely follow your own instincts. If you want to shut yourself away and be quiet, then just say 'I don't feel like seeing you today.' "

If you're feeling troubled and sad, get to a safe place. But what is a safe place? That doesn't always mean "group therapy." It could be a walk in the park, a sit in your favorite chair, a meal with people you're comfortable with.

I prefer the term "supportive environment." Letting go of troubles is not easy. It takes time. Some hurts, especially big ones, never go away. There will always be a hole in your heart.

Stages of Grief

Experiencing grief is not being a crybaby or wimp. Grief involves rage, anger and long term feelings of loss. Everyone experiences grief in his or her own way. There is no right or wrong way. Just as we all heal at different rates from illness or injury, we also heal at our own rate from emotional trauma. Some will heal faster than others. Be understanding of each other and give each other permission to grieve in his or her own way. Importantly, don't put a time-table on your grief.

And remember it is difficult to express grief, when society doesn't approve of or allow us to grieve.

Everybody experiences grief in his or her own way, but there are distinct stages of grief, as described by Dr. Elisabeth Kubler-Ross in her book, "On Death and Dying." (Macmillan Publishing, NY, 1969.)

You may have already experienced some of these stages, you may be experiencing some now, but all of them apply to you at some point. Do not be afraid of the grieving process. It's the mind's special way of dealing with trauma and loss. The more you resist the process, the longer it may take you to feel better—and feeling better is one of the most important things to work toward.

1) Protest. Emotions such as shock, confusion, denial, anger and lowered self-esteem take over. The feeling of

being numb is shock. Confusion may set in and make it difficult to concentrate or make decisions. There may be feelings of unfocused anger. You lash out at anyone or everything. How could this be happening to me? Physical and emotion symptoms include crying, pain, weakness, nausea, loss of appetite and sleep problems. As reality begins to set in, you start the next phase of the grief process, despair or sadness.

2) You feel extreme sadness. Anguish over what will never be for the animals. Anguish over having to continue killing animals. You may feel very tired. At times you may seem fine and then, for no apparent reason, the pain will wash over you like a wave of the ocean and knock you down. Even your dreams may be filled with the animals that are gone. There is a desire to stop trying so hard to do a good job. This is the next phase, detachment.

3) With detachment, apathy or not caring takes over. There is a loss of interest in many things. You may shut down while you are absorbing what is happening in your life. This stage leads to the final phase, recovery.

4) Recovery comes as you redefine some things in your life—specifically, your decision to enter the animal welfare field. You realize that things have changed for you: your ideas about some things, the way you view many things. You now realize that you can build a new reality and not have to forever mourn the old reality. You can choose to be forever sad or sad only when you need to be sad. You can choose to welcome life again.

The grief process may have to be repeated over and over again as you work through the daily or weekly routine of killing animals. The more you allow yourself to work through it, the easier it may become. Grief is a process and going through it is difficult, but in that process you will discover many things about yourself: that you are strong enough to acknowledge your losses and that you can successfully manage those losses.

How to Start a Support Group

Some agencies have begun to hold regularly scheduled euthanasia support groups. The purpose of a group is to provide an atmosphere of support and trust where feelings and emotions about euthanasia may be freely expressed. It is very important for the success of this type group that:

- The management support the entire process. This includes giving permission to hold the group(s) during working hours.

- The facilitators of the group be trained in Euthanasia Stress issues and the dynamics of group debriefing. It is not clear at this point if the facilitators should have a real hands-on experience with euthanasia to adequately empathize with the participants. It is vital that the facilitators understand their role with the group, that is, they are not therapists or counselors.

- An Employee Assistance Program be available to address any individual's need for counseling or therapy on life issues or extreme reactions to Euthanasia Stress.

- A regular schedule for the meetings be established to insure consistency and priority for the group participants.

- The rules of the group be clearly outlined, discussed and agreed on. This discussion should take place between the facilitator(s) and the management and between the facilitator(s) and participants.

- Questionnaires should be given to participants prior to starting the groups to determine any special needs that are present, such as how often do you euthanize, are there volunteers or non-euthanizing personnel that interfere with the process, do you work with the public, and so on.

Rules of the group should include:

- Understanding the purpose of the group. That is, to provide an environment where an individual can openly discuss personal and corporate issues concerning euthanasia of animals.

- Understanding that discussing euthanasia will be difficult due to the subject matter and that all participants will react and respond individually.

- Agreement that the support group is simply a source of support and validation to each other and that is not intended to solve personal problems, resolve employment conflicts or address extreme reactions to euthanasia. In any and all of these instances the individual must seek guidance from the appropriate professional.

- Agreement that participation in the group is strictly voluntary. That the employer is not requiring participation as a condition of employment.

- Agreement that the facilitator may ask a participant to seek guidance from a professional and can ask that a participant not attend if that individual is impeding the process for the others in the group.

- Agreement that permission will be given to all participants to express their feelings in an open and honest way. That no judgments will be made or condemnation given for open and honest expression of feelings. All participants must treat each other with respect and consideration.

- Agreement that above all else, all issues, whether personal or corporate, that are discussed in the group are to be kept totally confidential and are not to be discussed with anyone outside the group. This applies to the facilitator as well.

Finding a Facilitator

There may be several sources of facilitators for your Euthanasia Support group. Since Euthanasia Stress is starting to be recognized as a problem, many types of agencies are becoming involved.

Humane organizations connected to city and county governments could facilitate support groups through Employee Assistance Programs for its employees. These programs usually provide confidential counseling for a limited time at no charge to the employee. It is possible to arrange with the EAP to provide a counselor to facilitate support groups as part of the contract with the governmental agency or in addition to that contract for a small fee.

Check with the health insurance provider for your agency. Often the health insurance has some coverage for psychological counseling. It may be possible for the insurance company, as part of the coverage, to arrange for one of its providers to facilitate a support group.

Animal control and shelter agencies are often associated with, or part of, police departments. Many police departments have an auxiliary section called "victim assistance," "victim services," or "victim witness" programs. These programs provide trained personnel to assist citizens who have been involved in incidents which are usually of a violent nature (i.e., suicide, sexual assault, domestic violence, etc.). The program may be able to provide a member of that team to facilitate a support group.

Human Resources and Employee Relations departments often have personnel on staff with experience in debriefing groups and conflict resolution. Check with that department to see if there is anyone interested in facilitating a group.

In any of the above instances, it is important to obtain the support of the decision-making body of your organization to assist with these arrangements.

Employee Assistance Program Advice

"While it is easy to get caught up in the emotional and political issues surrounding euthanasia, it is also easy to overlook or ignore the feelings of ACOs and ETs who must perform the task. We don't want to know the person beneath the 'executioner's hood.' We'd rather they remain nameless and faceless and not share their thoughts and feelings about their jobs, not even with friends or family members. When confronted unexpectedly with the truth of their jobs, we often blurt out, 'I could never do your job—I care too much for animals, as though there is a difference between 'them and us.' "

From: EAP Digest (Sept./Oct. 1992) *Animal Control Workers: Ordinary People: Extraordinary Stresses* by David H. Schroeder, Ph.D.

Feelings, Emotions

EAP Advice from Dr. Schroeder, workplace wellness expert in California:

- ACO and ET training should include assurance that emotional reactions to euthanasia are normal and accepted. The ability to vent and share feelings and frustrations must be a built-in part of the job.

- Working to increase public awareness of the problems surrounding euthanasia helps the employee avoid taking on the guilt and stigma shoved their way.

- Everyone who works in a shelter—administrators, support staff and volunteers—should observe or be exposed to euthanasia. This helps break down the isolation of those who perform euthanasia regularly.

- Euthanasia is frequently performed by the newest or lowest paid staff member. Anything which upgrades the status of ETs helps legitimize their needs and complaints.

- ETs frequently need time to prepare for and come away from the task of euthanasia. This should be allowed and should not be considered idle or wasted time. The time of day euthanasia is scheduled also may be a concern to some ETs.

- Physical surroundings and hygiene measures can influence how the task is perceived. There's a big difference between working in a back room or shed and performing the service in a clinic-like atmosphere.

- Those who perform euthanasia benefit from sharing with others who understand their situation. The chance to attend meetings and have contact with other ETs can provide a support network for dealing with the emotional aspects of the job.

- Helping the spouses of ETs understand their mate's job also serves to break down isolation and expand the support network.

Stress Busters

Get in control of the things you can control. So many things are going to be out of control. But it's your responsibility to treat your own stress and recognize signs of burnout.

Ask yourself: How can I become more effective? How do I evaluate the amount of demands on my time at work and attend to my personal needs?

It could mean that sometimes there are things you might want to do, but if you try to do it all, you're going to make yourself less effective.

Determine what are the most important things you do and what are your limits.

Exercises for Individuals or Groups

Do you have trouble getting "in touch" with your feelings? Is it because you only have one feeling and that is called "numb"?

Here are a few activities that encourage communication and help people express their feelings. These can be done individually or in a group.

Fill in the Blank:

- The things that bother me about euthanasia are _____.

- The things that bug me about the public and its attitude towards euthanasia are_____.

- The public's perception of us is_____. For example: What are some of their typical comments? What are some of their reasons for surrender of animals?

Feelings, Emotions

- The characteristics of a Euthanasia Technician are _____.
- The things I do good at my job are_____.
- If I could say something to make the animals feel better, it would be_____.
- If I could do something special for myself, it would be _____.
- Some of the positive things I do for myself are_____.
- I can better meet my needs by_____.
- Something funny that happened to me was_____. For example: What makes you laugh? Is anything funny anymore?

Get the support you need and deserve!

Section 5:
Paws for Thought

Paws for Thought

Poems, Prayers and Editorials

Writing is a good way to express your feelings. This section contains some expressions written by and about animal care workers. So the next time you need to get something off your chest, try writing your own poem, journal entry or letter to the editor.

Abigail Van Buren, "Dear Abby," is the voice of common sense, reason and information. Her advice reaches millions of readers through her syndicated newspaper column. An Animal Control Officer sent in this item and it is now in her "Keepers" booklet.

Many thanks to Dear Abby and Universal Press Syndicate for granting permission to reprint the following columns.

Animal Control Officer
Seminole, Oklahoma

Dear Abby:
 I am your animal control officer. I am not the dreaded "dog catcher" or the "murderer" you call me. It is not I who allows your pet to roam the streets, to contract diseases from other free-roaming animals, to be hit by passing motorists or poisoned by rotting garbage. I am the one who must look into those sick, pain-glazed eyes, try to remove the animal without causing it further pain, and then humanely "put it to sleep" to put an end to its suffering.

 It is not I who allows your pet to breed, then dumps the unwanted puppies and kittens on roadsides and in shelters. I'm the one who must find the tiny animals before they die of starvation, exposure or disease, and as an act of mercy, exterminate them. It hurts me to be forced to kill hundreds of thousands of animals each year, but because of your irresponsibility, I have no choice.

 It is not I who abandons unwanted animals on farm roads, telling myself some friendly farmer will surely take them in and give them a good home. But I am the one who must pick up the frightened animal who waits in vain for its beloved master, wondering why it has been abandoned. I am the one who must help that friendly farmer trap, tranquilize or kill that animal because it has begun to roam in packs with other abandoned hungry animals, killing livestock, fowl and game.

I am not the one who breeds and fights dogs in the name of "sport." But I am the one who fights the breeders and participants, and must pick up the dead and dying animals that have been left behind.

It is not I who keeps a pet confined in an area too small—without food, water, shelter or exercise. But I must deal with the irresponsible owner who does.

It is not I who refuses to spend the time and money to keep up regular inoculations that all pets require. But I am the one who must pick up the sick animal who is dying of a preventable disease.

So remember, the next time your child is bitten by a stray dog, your trash is dumped and scattered, your pet is lost, stolen, poisoned or hit by a car, it is the animal control officer you call—not the "dog catcher." The next time your pet is picked up, or you are cited for neglecting or abusing it, remember, I am only trying to get you to fulfill your responsibility to your pet, your neighbor and yourself.

Do not scorn me. Respect me, for I am the product of your irresponsibility. I love animals and I care.

A Dog's Prayer
by Beth Norman Harris

Treat me kindly, my beloved master, for no heart in all the world is more grateful for kindness than the loving heart of me.

Do not break my spirit with a stick, for though I should

Poems, Prayers and Editorials

lick your hand between the blows, your patience and understanding will more quickly teach me the things you would have me do.

Speak to me often, for your voice is the world's sweetest music, as you must know by the fierce wagging of my tail when your footstep falls upon my waiting ear. When it is cold and wet, please take me inside, for I am now a domesticated animal, no longer used to bitter elements. And I ask no greater glory than the privilege of sitting at your feet beside the hearth. Though had you no home, I would rather follow you through ice and snow than rest upon the softest pillow in the warmest home in all the land, for you are my god and I am your devoted worshiper.

Keep my pan filled with fresh water, for although I should not reproach you were it dry, I cannot tell you when I suffer thirst. Feed me clean food, that I may stay well, to romp and play and do your bidding, to walk by your side, and stand ready, willing and able to protect you with my life should your life be in danger.

And, beloved master, should the Great Master see fit to deprive me of my health or sight, do not turn me away from you. Rather hold me gently in your arms as skilled hands grant me eternal rest...and I will leave you knowing with the last breath I drew, my fate was ever safest in your hands.

Taken from Dear Abby columns, by Abigail Van Buren.
©UNIVERSAL PRESS SYNDICATE. Reprinted with permission. All rights reserved.

Prayer for Animals
by Albert Schweitzer

Hear our humble prayer, O God
For our friends, the animals
Especially for animals who are suffering;
For all that must be put to death.
We entreat for them all thy mercy and pity.
And for those who deal with them,
We ask a heart of compassion, gentle and kindly words.
Make us true friends of the animals
And so to share the blessings of the merciful.

Kitten Season, Again
by Pat Miller

"Please tell me you won't kill them,"
the kittens' owner cried.
"I couldn't bear to tell the kids
that Fluffy's babies died!"

"Just look how wonderful they are,
all snuggled in their box...
One calico, one tiger-stripe,
one gray with four white socks."

"We promised when we got the cat
that we would get her spayed,
but we were just too busy;
the appointment got delayed."

"Before we even knew it
little Fluff was getting fat...
Pregnant at just six months old,
can you imagine that?"

"And then, of course, we realized
the kittens' lives were worth
the chance to let our kids enjoy
the miracle of birth."

"We tried real hard to find them
 homes
but it was pretty tough.
No one seemed to want to take
these precious balls of fluff."

She gave each kitten one last kiss
and left them with a sigh.
She missed the tear that trickled from the corner
of my eye.

I knew, like thousands come before
who had no better fared,
these kittens soon would die within
the arms of those who cared.

But as the lady reached the door
she turned and cleared her throat,
and against all crazy odds
my heart stood still with hope.

Perhaps she'd reconsidered
and perhaps she'd changed her mind.
Perhaps she knew she had a chance
to prove she could be kind.

But fleeting hopes were quickly
dashed;
reprieve was not to be,

for when she opened up her mouth
the lady said to me,

"Did I forget to tell you
that Fluffy's in the car?
We've decided we don't want
her either anymore."

reprinted from The California Humane Action and Information Network (C.H.A.I.N.)

Prayer of the Unborn

"I ask for the privilege of not being born...not to be born until you can assure me of a home and a master to protect me, and a right to live as long as I am able to enjoy life...not to be born until my body is precious and men have ceased to exploit it because it is cheap and plentiful."

Anonymous

Excerpt from a letter to the editor in NACA News:

"Dog catchers we are *NOT!* Animal Control Officers are professional, educated, devoted individuals. We will not be going away."

Darryl Heppner, Corona, California

True or False?

Humane societies protect animals from people.
Animal Control protects people from animals.

Shelter Worker's Credo

As animal shelter personnel with various duties and responsibilities, we hereby make the following promises and declarations:

- We hereby promise to love and to care for the pets brought into our shelter to the best of our ability.
- We promise to make them as comfortable as possible in an impossible situation.
- We promise to do our best to find them new homes.
- When all else fails, we promise to end their lives humanely in order to make room for the endless supply of animals to follow.

HOWEVER, we also stand firm with the following:

- We did not cause these animals to be born into this overpopulated world.
- We did not cause these pets to become a problem or inconvenience to their owners.
- We did not cause their owners to move, to have kids, to become allergic to them, or to become ill.
- We will not accept, nor allow to be placed on us, the guilt that belongs to the owners of these pets.

IT IS NOT OUR FAULT!

Written by Patti Judd, Euthanasia Technician at the Animal Welfare Association in Voorhees, New Jersey.

Reflections
by Barbara Hurst Smith, ©1979

Oh little one, you should not have been born
Into this world as an object to be torn
From a world of promises held out by mankind
Without the chance to grow, to seek, and to find.

As I stand looking into your puppy face
I mourn this act of deplorable waste
Your tiny mind senses that no one did care
Bewildered, rejected — you simply sit there
In a 3-by-2 cage you wait and you wait
Captive to an unknown and unjust fate.

No one came by or called to ask
If you were chosen in the days that passed.
Your mother once held out that promise "to be"
But your little eyes will never be able to see
The joy etched on a small child's face
Your furry warm body never feel an embrace.
Deprived of sharing in a child's golden hours
Never to run and prance amid spring showers
Never to fetch a ball or a stick
Never to be taught a doggie trick.
Never to be a mischievous pup
Only the pain of mankind's rebuff.
Never to smell the fragrance of summer flowery,
Euthanasia becomes your inherited dowry...
Never to chase whirling autumn leaves
Oh how these thoughts cause my heart to grieve.

Wagging tail
Trusting eyes

A puppy paw reaches out through the bar to me
Oh, dear God, if only we both could be free.
Free of the mental anguish, the emotional strain
This pup and I become as one in this senseless pain.

Who spun this thread of life?
Who determines the length?
Who decides the time?

APATHY dictates.
Oh little one, please understand—I love you,
And with love, I send you away.

      Amen.

You Are the Answer
by Barbara Hurst Smith, ©1979

Good morning, may we help you, is how we start our day.
"You won't kill them, will you?" are the first words you say.

They're female, mostly female, nine in this litter,
I gritted my teeth trying not to sound bitter.

You bring LIFE to us and briskly come in,
The novelty now faded with your whim.

You smile as you offer what to you seems a present,
We smile right back and try to be pleasant.

Your gift is our third since our office just opened,
We're your last resort—but you were just hoping

Paws for Thought

For a miracle—nine people to rush in
and choose each pup for a friend.

Our heart has grown heavy—our soul quite sad
You thought we would thank you and surely be
glad.

Glad to receive your careless mistake,
while you appear in six months for another retake.

We're a shelter, a place for unwanted animals,
where everyone loses when so many gamble.

Humane workers are desperate, weary, forlorn,
concerned for the millions that should not have been
born.

This is not what we wanted to be.
Please understand—don't you see? Won't you see?

You have made us a slaughterhouse of good will,
You must pause—consider what we feel.

The hurt that's inside because we do care
about those nine pups you have over there.

Bouncy and cuddly, cute—so much more,
But you only shrug as you walk out the door.

You left them for us to make the decision
which ones will die or go right on living.

Only one out of ten will be given a home
And for how long a time will she belong

To a family who chooses, for whatever reason
to return her to us because she's in season.

Poems, Prayers and Editorials

History repeats, for she will have been bred
She trembles it seems with fear and with dread.

The face of each worker can plainly be read
Because they know she will soon be dead.

We feel that we her more than you do,
There are so many, what else can we do?

You point your finger and say, "Oh the shame,
You put them to sleep, you are to blame."

Little do you realize how we try not to hate you,
And strive with much effort to educate you.

You didn't stay till the end to see us weep
When we had to take them and put them "to sleep."

Euthanasia—a kind death by definition,
Less birth would be kinder is our declaration!

But you go on your merry old way,
Forgetting too soon, and without much delay

That you caused the problem—YOU are the SOURCE
You just won't admit, of course.

We give our best for the animals and for you
Although the thank-yous are sparse and quite few.

Love and concern carry us through every day
We need your help! THERE MUST BE A BETTER WAY!

"Reflections" and "You Are the Answer" were reprinted with the permission of Bill Hurt Smith HSUS Animal Control Academy, Tuscaloosa, Alabama.

"Circle the Wagons, the Arrogant Are on the Warpath"
Editorial

Do you feel as though you are being attacked from all sides? For instance:

Animal Rightists demand the "Bill of Rights" cover all animal life.
Anti-vivisectionists state their way is the only way.
Vivisectionists state their way is the only way.
Vegetarians claim those who eat meat are destroying the environment.
Vegans call Vegetarians too liberal.
Hunters think those who oppose them are unbalanced.
Cattlemen want you to eat more meat.
Fur wearers are said to be cruel.
Trappers see no wrong in what they are doing.

The list goes on forever, it seems.

Most of the people in each of these categories appear to listen but their replies indicate they do not hear each other. This type of behavior is best described as arrogance (self importance). When you are so convinced that your beliefs are much more important than anyone who opposes you and therefore refuse to consider their beliefs, you are arrogant.

Name calling has become a ritual. Believers attack those who disagree with them as crazy, stupid, cruel, dishonest, wasteful, etc. This type of behavior is often defended as necessary if the believer is to make converts. After all, the First Amendment to the United States Constitution grants them the right to say anything to anybody at anytime. Correct? Correct.

Even strong supporters of the First Amendment occasionally give some thought to the Fourth Amendment (the right to privacy) and it would be nice if more of them did it more often.

"ALF"(Animal Liberation Front) is out there breaking into buildings and demonstrating a complete disregard for law and order. Until they surfaced, I thought ALF was a funny looking hairy thing on TV. Members of "ALF" and others of their ilk demand freedom for animals while they trample all over other people's rights.

It is very difficult for people who want what is best for all concerned to know what they should do. I've always been skeptical of those who verbally tell me one thing and their actions tell me another. Some animal rightists say they are against animal suffering at the hands of experimenters but they have been known to let animals continue to suffer while they document their case. And instances of proven cruelty by experimenters abound. The government, in some instances, has covered up these expensive and foolish experiments but the willful destruction of property by animal action groups causes the cost to climb higher.

Foolish animal experiments (apparently in the high percentiles) and the disregard of constitutional rights cannot be forgiven and must be discontinued. Two wrongs do not make a right! This is the United States. We believe in *debate* on any issue and majority rules. So debate and stop being criminals. Both sides of these issues should stop calling each other names, manufacturing statistics, making insupportable statements, committing crimes and generally acting like juvenile delinquents. Present your case calmly, honestly and passionately and the American Public will render its decision.

The people of this country will listen if you don't bullshit them. —*The Editor.*

The NACA News, National Animal Control Association
Indianola, Washington

A Great Moment at the Shelter
by Eddie Ladson
Columbia, South Carolina, Animal Services

Morning at the shelter can be so much fun
   as you listen to the puppies and watch them run.
You greet your fellow employees well,
   as stories of the day before they tell.
The cats meow as we speak,
   for they, too, know it's time to eat
I wash their pens and make them shine,
   you know I wish they were all mine.
The Persian cat loves to purr,
   The Siamese such lovely fur!
The orange tabby is oh so fat,
   The gray tabby is a mellow cat.
The black cat looks so cool and sleek,
   while the white cat sits calmly and eats.
We care for them as our own,
   and hope very soon they will have a home.

Section 6:
The Challenges Ahead

The Challenges Ahead

Survival: Burn Out or Rust Out?

What kind of human being is left working at a shelter after ten years? Who makes it past two years in the business?

Interestingly, it's often a myth that the only way you can last that long is by becoming cold and uncaring. A few have, but many have channeled their rage and grief by becoming cynical, hypercritical and even self-righteous.

By continually seeing the worst in human behavior, they have lost faith in people.

On the other extreme, are the longtime shelter employees who are rusting out on the job. Nothing seems to bother them one way or the other. They are simply marking time until retirement.

For the animals' sake, don't let this happen to you!

For the humane movement's sake, don't let this happen!

For the sake of your own spirit and emotional well-being, don't give in to either condition.

Carter Luke, Vice President and Euthanasia Consultant at the Massachusetts Society for the Prevention of Cruelty to Animals has survived 17 years in this business. He admits it's a challenge to stay fresh and motivated all the time, but he is determined not to give up.

"I don't consider uncaring people effective. If you be-

come too comfortable with euthanasia so that it doesn't affect you, you've lost an edge," he says. "Because euthanasia is not an acceptable solution to pet overpopulation. We should always see it as something we abhor, and wish to get rid of or at least minimize. We should never become comfortable with euthanasia."
But it will be with us for a while.

You need to be good at euthanasia, you need to study it and get the best training you can, he adds, but he believes the euthanasia staff should be rotated. That's for a couple of reasons. One, it's helpful for the whole staff to have a better personal understanding of this phenomenon we call euthanasia. And two, we all need a break, because we shouldn't only see the negative side of dealing with unwanted animals.

Dealing With the Public

It doesn't serve our movement to blame and humiliate people, continues Luke.

"I believe I can make a difference, if I can find the key to open their door. We are all teachers. We must create an atmosphere that allows people to learn. You can't say to a person who comes into your shelter: 'Hey Jerk! You're a stupid and irresponsible person. You'll never get a dog from me!' And then think you can teach them something? You're dreaming.

"What I'm saying, is in the shelter, even if you are facing someone who has committed an irresponsible act you must treat them with respect.

"Generally, everyone in the world thinks they are responsible and basically kind. We need to learn how to differentiate between an act of irresponsibility that someone *does* and whether or not that *person* is irresponsible or uncaring. I believe that a lot of irresponsible acts are done purely due to ignorance or not thinking."

Don't give up on people

Luke believes most people are basically good. "But, for either unthinking or foolish reasons, they commit irresponsible acts or even acts that cause suffering. But that doesn't mean that they are sadistic or evil people. That's the paradox we're in. We often see the worst of people. And that's the challenge of staying in this business."

Grief Resolution

Being able to resolve your grief is another factor for surviving in this business, Luke says.

"We should always maintain a certain degree of grieving and resolve the personal emotional aspect to take care of ourselves and to be able to carry on."

It's not easy. It takes work. You can't ignore it. But you can turn that grief and rage into something constructive for yourself, the movement and for the animals. That's why, in order to be effective, you must take care of yourself.

"Especially when I know I have to go into the Euthanasia Room and kill 35 healthy, young beautiful kittens. And then I'm going to go to the shopping mall with my humane society display and educate people. I have to be able to resolve my grief and leave my frustration and anger in the Euthanasia Room and be able to go to the mall and be an effective teacher.

"I know I'm going to cry from time to time. I need to

cry. I know I'm going to get angry. I need to get angry. And that's OK. As long as I can work through it emotionally and put the experience into a useful channel, I will not mask the outrage. People need to know the truth. But my own emotional agenda is not the issue. The needs of animals are the focus of my attention and my work.

"If I don't grieve it is just sitting in there stewing inside of me. I have to allow myself that experience. It has to be a motivating factor for me to want to make positive changes rather than negative changes in my own head. That kind of thinking frequently can lead some people to lash out at the world. That will never solve anything."

Rewards

But you must find rewards. "People who deal with negative things like euthanasia need to enjoy positive relationships with animals," continues Luke. "We have to be able to feel and see that we are making a difference. We can remember the animals that we *did* put an extra effort in. The ones that *did* survive, the animal that *did* go to a wonderful home. We can remember the incredible positive long term gain of talking with a group of kids, of speaking to people at malls and fairs. Every time we make arrangements to help someone have their animals spayed or neutered. That's a victory."

Also, Luke thinks an animal shelter from time to time should take on a special case. That could mean helping an injured dog. It helps the shelter, and the public sees there is positive value to the humane work that we do. These are the kinds of constructive actions that directly help reduce the number of unwanted animals killed.

We *have* made a difference

It's a very different world out there for animal shelters than it was just five years ago. The public expectations of us are a lot different than they were five years ago. It's a challenge for us not to say, that's how we did it in 1985 or 1978.

Luke believes we have made some dents in people's mindsets. More people than ever before are aware of the needs, the intrinsic value and the worth of animals. "I feel very good about that. I feel as though myself and the organizations I have worked for are starting to make that dent. We still have a lot of work to do, but I don't feel as if we are talking in a foreign language when we come into a school room and talk about responsible pet ownership. For the first time, high school classrooms, college classes and vet schools, are talking about issues that relate to the relationship between animals and the environment. We've become much more sensitized as a culture to those issues and that makes me feel good."

How we all respond to this work is very personal. We have to think about it, we have to talk about it, and then each of us comes to our own conclusion about it.

When will this suffering end?

There are no easy answers. Only challenges for those of us committed to animal protection and welfare.

The pet overpopulation crisis will not be over soon. Shelters will not be going out of business for lack of animals to control and house. I believe that is a legitimate fear of some people in animal control. Especially county and city-controlled shelters that are already understaffed, under

The Challenges Ahead

budgeted and at the mercy of government handouts. Education is one of the most effective tools we have to work with to prevent cruelty to animals. In recent years, there has been a growing awareness of the problem of unwanted animals. But more has to be done and tougher actions are needed. In March 1993, The Humane Society of the United States called for a Voluntary Breeding Moratorium on cats and dogs.

"We have to have an end in sight," says Marc Paulhus, HSUS Vice President for Companion Animals concerning the voluntary breeding moratorium. "We have to be far more aggressive. We are sick of putting healthy unwanted animals to death."

The Voluntary Breeding Moratorium is absolutely necessary. Spay/neuter programs are making a significant difference but there is still such a tremendous oversupply of cats and dogs in this country. Until the situation does get better, the euthanasia cycle will continue.

"Our job is not to pick them up and kill them," says Paulhus. "Our job is to be part of the solution. We don't want an end to kittens and puppies. We want to put an end to the euthanizing of millions of healthy animals."

From NACA News November/December, 1992:

> "Animal control personnel work endlessly to overcome public ignorance and misconceptions regarding all aspects of responsible pet ownership, from licensing and neutering to keeping animals at home and under control. We must do everything possible to educate the public.
>
> "We can't expect 100 percent compliance with the

Voluntary Breeding Moratorium, especially with those Americans who believe it is their constitutional right to overbreed, abuse and neglect animals."

ET Certification Curriculum

A big project that should be unveiled by the end of 1993 involves The Humane Society of the United States and the American Humane Association.

The groups have been working together to produce a single book outlining animal shelter euthanasia services that are practical, cost-effective and legal for animal shelters, but consistent with the American Veterinary Medical Association guidelines released in January 1993.

"This report will be far more detailed than anything any of the organizations have independently produced so far," explains Paulhus. "It will outline what we find acceptable for shelters to provide humane and painless death to animals. Our book will address the whole issue of how euthanasia should be conducted in a shelter."

The goal is to mandate certification in every state and tie that in with legislation that will allow shelters direct purchase of sodium pentobarbital.

Another goal of the project is to develop uniform standards for Euthanasia Technician training and certification and re-certification in all 50 states.

"I think we will need an initial training and certification course, followed by annual recertification," says Paulhus. "Recertification would not involve the degree of initial ET training, but would be done to make sure the person retains the knowledge and proficiency to justify recertification."

Role of Animal Shelters in the Future

Humane societies are moving away from the traditional role of simply providing humane shelter and death for the animals they take in.

"We've still got to do this, but we've also got to focus more on why animals are coming to us, not just on what happens to them when they get here," says Joe Silva, Director of Shelters at the Massachusetts Society for the Prevention of Cruelty to Animals in *Animals Magazine*.

A variety of innovative programs benefit animals, shelter workers and the communities they serve. Public education is the key to the animal overpopulation problem. Mandatory spay/neuter laws and breeding bans are making a difference in the pet overpopulation problem, but there's still much to be done to make pet sterilization standard practice.

Unwanted litters are not the only shelter arrivals. Abuse also plays a role in needless animal deaths and public outreach can help prevent this as well. An MSPCA survey showed that lack of time and failure to consider the needs of animals before acquiring them were frequent reasons for owners surrendering cats and dogs.

Shelters of the future will be devoting as much energy and effort on educating people, as on cleaning and feeding animals. And hopefully euthanasizing fewer animals.

Honor the Animals—and Yourself

Rituals can have a profound affect on our lives. We can't have funeral services for each and every animal. Some ETs, however, say a silent prayer for each animal they euthanize.

Others pray for strength and hope that the situation will get better.

The line "With love, I send you away" in Barbara Smith's "Reflections" says so much. I always feel a tug at my heart when I hear those words.

In 1992 animal groups throughout the country participated in a candlelight vigil known as "Homeless Animals' Day." People gathered to speak out on the pet overpopulation crisis, sing songs, read poems and pray in memory of the unwanted animals. The event provided an opportunity for people to express their feelings and join forces with other animal organizations.

No one wants to eliminate dogs and cats, we just want to eliminate their suffering. And, ultimately, eliminate the stress and suffering of the Euthanasia Technician.

Ten Rational Plans of Action for the Pet Overpopulation Crisis

- Take an activist stand for animal welfare.
- Demand humane treatment and sanitary conditions for laboratory research animals.
- Demand that all animals are spayed/neutered before leaving the shelter. Support the HSUS voluntary breeding moratorium.
- Demand that animal shelters exist not only for the good of its animals, but take care of its employees.
- Know how to talk to the media. Be articulate. Know where you stand.
- Don't let a few animal rights crazies speak against you or bash your shelter.
- Know who your supporters are. Recognize your supporters. Thank them.
- Go into the schools and speak on humane education.
- Provide a humane death with dignity for the unwanted, abandoned, unadoptable animals.
- Realize one person *can* make a difference.

Section 7:
Resource Guide

Resource Guide

Knowledge is powerful. I think it's important to study all sides of an issue. Here are a variety of sources.

Consultants on Euthanasia Stress

Phil Arkow, Education and Publicity Director
Humane Society of the Pikes Peak Region
633 S. 8th Street
Colorado Springs, CO. 80901
(719) 473-1741
   Conducts "Coping with the Stress of Euthanasia" and "Who Cares for the Caregivers?"

Doug Fakkema
Route 3, Box 3583
Washburn, WI 54891
(715) 373-5219
   Conducts workshops, training and crisis intervention

Carter Luke, Vice President, Humane Services Division
MSPCA
350 S. Huntington Avenue
Boston, MA 02130
(617) 522-4885

Resource Guide

Bill Hurt Smith, Consultant
4210 Springhill Drive
Tuscaloosa, AL 35405
(205) 553-9752
  Conducts euthanasia workshops

Karen Stickland
Harrison Memorial Animal Hospital
191 Yuma Street
Denver, CO 80223
(303) 722-2100, x319
  Conducts support groups for ETs

Doug Kelly, Supervisor
Lakewood Animal Control
445 S. Allison Parkway
Lakewood, CO 80226-3105
(303) 987-7123
  Conducts support groups for ETs

Dennis Fetko, Ph.D. "Dr. Dog"
P.O. Box 28176
San Diego, CA 92198
(619) 485-7433
  Conducts seminars, sells audio and video tapes

Tom Colvin, Director
Animal Rescue League of Iowa
5452 NE 22nd Street
Des Moines, IA 50313
  Directs euthanasia school each year at Iowa State University with Ron Grier, DVM, Ph.D., professor of Veterinary Clinical Sciences

Pat Hubbard
Cedar Valley Humane Society
7411 Mt. Vernon Road SE
Cedar Rapids, IA 52403
(515) 362-6288

Dr. C.M. Towers
The Midwest Academy Humane Society/Animal Control
Eastside Veterinary Clinic
999 44th Street
Marion, IA 52302
(319) 373-1908
   Conducts annual nonprofit animal control academy

Tim Greyhavens
Washington Progressive Animal Welfare Society
15305 44th Avenue West
Linwood, WA 98037
(206) 742-4142, x 876

Diedre Young, Euthanasia Technician
Euthanasia Hotline
Benton, AR 72015
(501) 778-7401

Randall Lockwood, Ph.D.
Humane Society of the U.S.
2100 L Street NW
Washington, DC 20037
(202) 452-1100
   ET certification training and information

Reference Material

Animal Euthanasia
Special Reference Briefs, USDA
National Agricultural Library
Beltsville, MD 20705
(301) 344-3755

Euthanasia Guide, $12
by Dr. Ron Grier and Tom Colvin
Dept. of Veterinary Clinical Science
Iowa State University
Ames, IA 50011
(515) 294-4900

Handbook of Pentobarbital Euthanasia, $8.50
Tim Greyhavens
Humane Society of the Willamette Valley
P.O. Box 13005
Salem, OR 97309

Criteria for Selection of Animals for Euthanasia
Animal Rescue League of Boston
Tom White, Director of Operations
P.O. Box 265
Boston, MA 02117
  Write for a free copy of criteria.

1993 Report of the AVMA Panel on Euthanasia JAVMA, Vol. 202, No. 2, Jan. 15, 1993

Bibliography

Arkow, Phil, "The Humane Society and the Human-Companion Animal Bond," The Humane Society of the Pikes Peak Region, Colorado Springs, CO.

Arluke, Arnold, "Coping With Euthanasia: A Case Study of Shelter Culture," JAVMA, Vol. 198, No. 7, April 1, 1991.

Arluke, Arnold, "Trapped in a guilt cage," New Scientist, April 1992.

Owens, Charles E., Ricky Davis and Bill Hurt Smith, "The Psychology of Euthanizing Animals: The Emotional Components," (Int. I Stud Anim Prob, 1981.)

Animal Shelter Reporting Study, 1990, research shows reduction of euthanasia with increased spay/neuter programs, $10. American Humane Association, 63 Inverness Drive East, Englewood, CO 80112.

Palmer, C. Eddie, "The Working Personality of the Animal Control Officer," Centaur: The Journal of Human/Animal Interface, Spring 1992.

Rollin, Bernard E., Ph.D., "Euthanasia and Moral Stress," Professor of Philosophy and Department of Physiology and Biophysics, Colorado State University, Fort Collins, CO 80523.

Books & Publications

After Great Pain, a New Life Emerges. Diane Cole. Summit Books, New York: 1992.

The Animal Rights Crusade: The Growth of a Moral Protest. James M. Jasper and Dorothy Nelkin. The Free Press, New York: 1992.

Being Kind to Animal Pests. A no-nonsense guide to humane animal control with cage traps. Steve Meyer, P.O. Box 247, Garrison, IA 52229.

Resource Guide

Never Let Them See You Cry. Edna Buchanan, Random House, New York, 1992.

Crazy Dogs & Crazy People. Looking at Behavior in Our Society. C.W. Meisterfeld, Canine Psychoanalyst and Ernest Pecci, M.D., Psychiatrist. MRK Publishing, 448 Seavey, Petaluma, CA 94951.

On Death and Dying. Elisabeth Kubler-Ross. Macmillan Publishing, New York: 1970.

The Forbidden Zone. Michael Lesy. Anchor/Doubleday, New York: 1989. Interviews with people who work around death.

Forever Friends, Resolving Grief After the Loss of a Beloved Animal. Joan Coleman. J.C. Tara Enterprises, Inc., 3230 E. Flamingo Rd., Suite 276, Las Vegas, NV 89121.

The Hijacking of the Humane Movement. Rod and Patti Strand. Doral Publishing, P.O. Box 596, Wilsonville, OR 97070.

Inhumane Society, the American Way of Exploiting Animals. Dr. Michael W. Fox. St. Martin's Press, New York: 1990.

Save the Animals! 101 Easy Things You can Do. Ingrid Newkirk. National Director, People for the Ethical Treatment of Animals(PETA). Warner Books, New York: 1990.

Working From the Heart. For those who hunger for meaning and satisfaction in their work. Jacqueline McMakin with Sonya Dyer. LuraMedia, 7060 Miramar Road, Suite 104, San Diego, CA 92121.

Animals Magazine, MSPCA
350 South Huntington Avenue
Boston, MA 02130

Animal People
P.O. Box 205
Shushan, NY 12873

Wildlife Rehabilitation Today
Coconut Creek Publishing Co.
2201 NW 40th Terrace
Coconut Creek, FL 33066-2032
(305) 972-6092

Video

"Attitudes on Euthanasia" $45
HSUS
2100 L St. NW
Washington, DC 20037
 Narrated by the late Phyllis Wright, discusses the emotional difficulties faced by the workers; offers suggestions for coping; shows the proper way to handle animals that are going to be euthanized in order to minimize stress for them.

Organizations & Resource People

American Humane Association
63 Inverness Drive East
Englewood CO 80112
(303) 792-9900

Resource Guide

The Humane Society of the U.S.
2100 L Street NW
Washington, DC 20037
(202) 452-1100

National Animal Control Association
P.O. Box 1600
Indianola WA 98342
(800)828-6474

Animal Welfare Information Center
National Agricultural Library
10301 Baltimore Boulevard
Beltsville, MD 20705

American Veterinary Medical Association
1931 North Meacham Road, Suite 100
Schaumburg, IL 60173
(708) 925-8070; 1-800-248-2862

National Wildlife Rehabilitators Association
Carpenter Nature Center
12805 St.Croix Trail
Hastings, MN 55033
(612) 437-9194

International Wildlife Rehabilitation Counsel
4437 Central Place Suite B-4
Suisin, CA 94585
(707)864-1761

Wildlife Rescue and Sanctuary
105 North S Street
Pensacola, FL 32505
(904) 433-9453

Ken Wolff, Director
Grounded Eagle Foundation
Star Route 900
Condon, MT 59826
(406)754-2880

For information on humane trapping of feral cats and animal pests:

Dave Pauli, Regional Director
HSUS, Northern Rockies Regional Office
Transwestern II, Suite 315
490 North 31st Street
Billings, MT 59101
(406) 255-7161

Animal Protection Institute of America
Bob Hillman, Field Services Director
P.O. Box 22505
Sacramento, CA 95822

SPCA of Monterey County
Kevin Kraynak, Human Resource Manager
P.O. Box 3058
Monterey, CA 93942
(408) 373-2631, x228
  Conducts regular Euthanasia Stress and grief support groups for its employees

ASPCA
424 East 92nd Street
New York, NY 10128
(212) 876-7700

Resource Guide

Spay USA
P.O. Box 801
Trumbull, CT 06611
(800) 248-SPAY

Animal Organizations & Services Directory
3004 Maple Ave.
Manhattan Beach, CA 90266

The Fund for Animals
200 West 57th Street
New York, NY 10019
(212) 246-2096

Ira Slotkin, MSW, MA Ed.
Pet Loss Consulting Services
1212 Castle Hill #14
Austin TX 78703
(512) 478-8065
 Conducts workshops for Euthanasia Stress and grief

Psychologists for the Ethical Treatment of Animals (PSYeta)
P.O. Box 1297
Washington Grove, MD 20880

The Association of Veterinarians for Animal Rights
P.O. Box 6269
Vacaville, CA 95696

In Defense of Animals
816 West Francisco Blvd.
San Rafael, CA 94901
(415) 453-9984
 Investigates and exposes instances of abuse

Paws for Thought

Responsible Dog Owners Association
P.O. Box 173
Fountainville, PA 18923
(215) 249-1377

The Delta Society
P.O. Box 1080
Renton, WA 98057
(206) 226-7357

Glossary

I have talked to dozens of animal control officers and volunteers across the country. Many did not know what some of these terms meant or were afraid to ask. To me, it emphasizes the importance of education, job training and open communication.

Animal care attendant: doesn't this job title sound better than kennel clerk?

Animal fundamentalists; animal rights advocates, believe animals should live their lives without human interference.

Animal pests: creatures who cross our paths in search of food or shelter. This is considered to be a more sensitive term than "nuisance wildlife."

Animal pragmatists: believe that animals deserve moral consideration, but maintain a balance between human and animal interests.

Animal welfarists: believe that animals deserve compassion and protection. They avoid cruelty and work to avoid unwanted animal populations.

Anthropomorphism, anthropomorphic, anthropomorphize: to attribute human behavior or human characteristics to animals. Many people believe animals, especially dogs and cats think like humans do.

Civilians: Them. People who work on the other side of the kennel fence. Could be family, friends or other co-workers.

Convenience euthanasia: or "paid euthanasia" or owner requested euthanasia. Requested by pet owners at their convenience on a healthy animal they are surrendering.

Collectors: people, who, bless their hearts, believe they are helping animals, but actually encourage overbreeding and disease in strays by only feeding them.

D Zone: the Disquieted Zone, a term coined by Bill Smith, HSUS instructor and frequent workshop leader on euthanasia. It refers to the troubled state of mind experienced by people who are faced with the conflicts of euthanasia.

Dumping: a technique used by so-called "no-kill" shelters; as in "dumping" the unhealthy, elderly animals on "kill" shelters which are left to determine the animals' fate.

Euthanasia: the act of inducing the painless death of an animal, from the Greek word meaning "good death." Using the term "humane euthanasia" is redundant, like saying "good death good death."

Feral: existing in a wild or untamed state.

Fractious: a domestic or feral animal that resists handling or approach.

Furry people syndrome: see Anthropomorphism.

Lassie syndrome: people who, upon acquiring a dog assume the canine is born trained. If it's a collie, then it must be as smart as Lassie.

Misanthrope, misanthropic: a person who hates or distrusts mankind; people haters.

Nuisance wildlife: a term used to describe animals that cross our paths as we both go about our lives. In the animal's case, the creature is usually seeking food or shelter. Although they may be considered a "nuisance," be humane. A more sensitive term to use would be "animal pests."

No-kill shelter: the operators, usually supported entirely by donations, mean well, but are usually not honest with themselves about the suffering caused to animals, by their isolation and lack of care. Sometimes called "pet mini-warehouses" or "concentration camps for cats and dogs."

Glossary

Pet of the week people: pet owners who acquire animals, but never manage to hold on to the animals more than a week or a few months at most. The animals usually wander off or get run over.
Puppy mills: an intensive breeding operation which HSUS estimates churns out about 500,000 animals a year in the U.S. Greedy operators breed as many dogs as space permits; as often as biologically possible. Veterinary care, nutritional needs and human attention are frequently ignored or barely tended to.
Sin-eater: someone who gets blamed for, takes the blame of society, in many ways, that is why shelter workers are considered "sin-eaters." Society and the public wants to dump their guilt with their unwanted animals on you.
Selectively humane: see dumping.
Surrender: the act of leaving unwanted animals at a shelter.
Zoological garbage collector: term used by sociologist, Dr. C. Eddie Palmer to describe animal control officers.

About the Author

B.J. Ellis graduated from Southern Methodist University in Dallas, Texas, with a B.F.A. in 1972.

An award-winning writer and former newspaper reporter, she has written numerous articles in magazines such as "Family Circle," "Good Dog!," "Wildlife Conservation" and others. Her articles have appeared in newspapers throughout the country and in Canada. She has written articles for AHA's "Shoptalk" and her photographs have appeared in HSUS's "Shelter Sense."

This is her first book.

Ms. Ellis is committed to working for solutions to the pet overpopulation crisis but even more concerned about the way society and the media treat animal shelters and its employees.

Ms. Ellis is a member of The Humane Society of the United States, American Humane Association, the Delta Society, American Society for the Prevention of Cruelty to Animals, the National Animal Control Association and the International Wildlife Rehabilitation Counsel. A portion of this book's proceeds will be donated to establish a "Wellness and Recognition" Fund and award for animal welfare workers.

Please feel free to write Ms. Ellis c/o:

Paw Print Press
7509-I Garners Ferry Road, Suite 164
Columbia, SC 29209

ORDER FORM

PAWS FOR THOUGHT

A Look at the Conflicts, Questions and Challenges of Animal Euthanasia

— B.J. Ellis —

Only $9.95 each when you order more than 1!	AMOUNT DUE
☐ Please send me 1 book ($12.95)	
☐ Please send me ___ books ($9.95 each)	
☐ I am a SC resident (add 5% sales tax)	
Shipping and handling are included **TOTAL**	

SHIP TO:

_____
Name

_____
Organization

_____
Address

_____
City   *State*   *Zip*

_____
Phone (include area code)

Send a check or money order (sorry, no C.O.D.) to:

PAW PRINT PRESS
c/o B.J. Ellis
7509-I Garners Ferry Road, Suite 164
Columbia, South Carolina 29209